THE TRUMP CHRONICLES: Volume One

By Mike Donovan

This book was all written in real time. It is a record of events and opinions from the time Trump announced for president in 2015 until August of 2017.

At first (the second entry in the book) I liked him, and for about three weeks he had my support. That tells you a lot about me. Most Trump-haters never liked him a tiny bit, not even for one day. The man had my support, but then lost it.

Most of this book is more or less the Diary of a Trump-hater, however, I occasionally side with him, and against his critics. Not very often mind you, but enough to separate me from most of the Trump-haters out there.

I don't argue on the internet, and I almost never share my political opinions there. I save it up for a book. If you want my opinion you can buy the book.

4

Many people have said that they would like to punch Donald Trump in the nose. These types of sentiments are often expressed here, and in the crassest way possible.

However, it is just venting, and figurative speech. The last thing in the world I really want is for any actual harm to come to my president, not matter how much I may hate him, and in spite of some things I suggest in here that I would like to see happen to him.

I am saddened, to say the least, to see people in 2020 actually commenting in public that they hope Trump gets coronavirus. I would never ever wish that on my president.

Aside from the angry opinions, I am also compiling an interesting chronicle of the current events of the time. It's easy to forget things. Call him what you will, (and I do) Trump is never boring! You will definitely read some of this and say, "Oh yeah, I forgot about that one." It's a useful recap, even if you hate some of my opinions.

In 2020, angry demonstrators attacked the White House and tried to push the fence down. President Trump was evacuated to an emergency shelter in the basement. The Trump-haters have been gloating over this, calling him, "Bunker Bitch."

As far as I'm concerned, all bets are off. I won't say I like him, but when you attack my president, you attack me, you attack my flag, and you attack the rule of law. I wish I could be on his security team. I'd take a bullet in the chest to protect him (but not one in the dick.)

I've never felt less hatred for this man that I have lately, even though I agree with the critics that he has handled the Covid-19 epidemic very poorly. I just feel very defensive when a mob attacks the White House. How about a little respect!

I loved Reagan, didn't like Jimmy Carter, like the Bushes, liked Obama, and hate Trump. I am inconsistent with my opinions because I have no agenda. I am not a crusader for the left or the right. I am not politically correct but I don't strive to be politically incorrect either. Sometimes I am politically correct, and sometimes I'm not. I take everything on a case by case basis, and I am always ready to change my mind about things and about people.

The Trump Chronicles, Volume One

CHURCH SHOOTING IN SC - JUNE 2015

A young racist white man went into a South Carolina Church and shot 8 black people to death during a prayer meeting. The entire nation was upset by this one.

Of course the first thing a lot of people said was that he was suffering from "mental illness." I agree with an article saying they were sick of giving vile racists a free automatic pass under the title, "mental illness." Anyone who decides on murder can be said to be "suffering from mental illness." Giving racists a pass on this count is a national mental illness.

This ill man was actually kicked out of the American Nazi Party for being too violent. That's about all you need to know about him.

He said he wanted to start a race war. In the reaction there was a great outpouring of racial harmony instead. 'Black and white together' church ceremonies were held in 50 states.

Meanwhile, in a related item, a national debate continues about whether the Confederate Battle Flag is offensive and should be removed from Southern state capitals and license plates. Walmart is removing all Confederate Battle Flag items from their shelves.

TRUMP CARD - JUNE 2015

Billionaire Donald Trump has announced his candidacy for president. My liberal pal called me to talk about how bad it was, and I didn't doubt him. I decided to clean my room while playing the speech in the background. I expected to hate his speech because I never liked him. But the speech wasn't bad at all. A few things caught my ear and made me smile. He pointed out that he was so rich he was one of the few politicians that couldn't be bought. Good point. But mostly I liked the way he talked about taking care of business in the Middle East with regard to the ISIS crisis.

TRUMP SURGE - JULY 2015

Donald Trump took the lead in the Republican race for the presidential nomination in July. At the end of the month he still held it. A lot of people were shocked. He is the most hated candidate in the field, yet he had a 12 point lead over Jeb Bush in the New Hampshire polls, and trails Scott Walker by 17 to 19 in Iowa polls. The left wing media is beside itself trying to call him vicious names and all they do is grow the monster.

Everyone thought Trump was through when he had the nerve to take a cheap shot at Vietnam War hero John McCain.

"He's a war hero because he was captured. I like people who don't get captured, okay?" said Trump.

Sacrilege!

I agree that it was a low blow cheap shot, but on the other hand I found it refreshing at the same time that he doesn't seem to give a damn. Trump wouldn't apologize for the remark. *The Des Moines Register* ran an editorial calling on Trump to resign from the race for the comment. As if that would ever happen! Trump responded by banning *DMR* reporters from his rallies and press conferences!

Interestingly, a *Boston Globe* article 10 days later reported that the veterans were mixed in their reaction. Some were offended, but many vets felt that McCain may be a hero but he does not do enough to help the vets, and that he's all about McCain and no one else. I happen to agree with that. Also, some Vietnam PW's actually expressed relief that someone finally had the nerve to say that. These ex-PW's told the

Globe reporter that they never felt like heroes for being prisoners of war. They always felt uncomfortable with people calling them heroes and they didn't resent Trump for speaking his mind.

People clearly like the idea that Trump doesn't apologize even if he is out of line a bit now and then. All these politicians walking on egg shells all the time, being only concerned with not saying anything that might cause a stir and get them in trouble, they get really tiresome. For Trump to come along and boldly tweak the sacrosanct McCain did not really hurt Trump that much at all. It might have even helped him, even if he was wrong. Many veterans feel that a President Trump will look out for their interests better than McCain ever has to date. And on immigration, McCain is a big time equivocator, while Trump comes down solidly on getting tough and building a giant wall on the southern border.

Even though he leads in the July 2015 polls and is worth more than 10 billion dollars, pundits keep asking if Trump can sustain this. Is he a fluke? Will he drop like a rock after the first debates?

What is weird to me is that no one seems to see all his money as anything but a novelty. I remember Mondale when he lost to Reagan in 1984 talking about how "The Republicans outspent us." Many candidates that lose the election talk of being "outspent" by their opponent. We had the better message, but they had the better bankroll, goes the gripe.

Well if there is anything to that complaint, then why don't the experts factor that in when assessing Trumps chances to stay in the race?

Don's the front runner, and is running neck and neck with Hillary Clinton in the national polls. He is ahead of Jeb Bush by a slim margin, has more than 10 BILLION dollars to play with, enough to outspend the entire Democratic Party, and all I keep hearing from the political gurus is the theoretical question: "Can he sustain this? - Is he a viable candidate, or is he just a fluke?"

Last time I checked, the front runner is the front runner. I hated Trump a year ago, I have to say as of now, he has my vote. I haven't been this excited about a candidate running for president in a long time, maybe never in my lifetime. All my lefty friends hate him so much they can't hear his name without posting an internet tirade full of vulgar name calling, as if that contributes anything to intelligent political discourse.

I know one thing. He talks my language when it comes to dealing with the threat of fundamental Islamic terrorism. I don't agree with Trump on all the issues and I'm middle of the road on immigration. I'm torn. I see both left and right on it and can't decide. But when it comes to the racist, sexist, xenophobic, regressive, fundamental Muslim radicals, I plan to vote for who is most likely to go over there and smash them to bits with US military power. Right now, Trump is the only one who is at least talking the talk.

Of course, if Trump wins, he will have a hard time getting Congressional support for his tough policies. But at least he is talking the talk I want to hear.

I've never been more annoyed with Obama than I am these days. He seems unsure of himself. Every press conference he reaches to criticize his Republican critics and does so in a stammering, unsure, reaching slowly for his careful choice of words, sort of way. Obama doesn't slam dunk his statements like he is unafraid. It takes him 2 minutes to say one sentence explaining why this critic or that critic is bad for America. Spit it out, sir. Speak your mind! Trump may be wrong on a lot of things, but at least he speaks without fear. He is the most non-boring serious contender I have ever seen in a Presidential race. I'd put a Trump bumper sticker on my Buick but I can't afford to get my car windows smashed in right now. I live in Massachusetts.

I've tried so hard to like Obama, but this business of never even saying that the enemy is 'fundamental Islamic terrorism' has a lot of people very angry. The cities and towns in Iraq that US soldiers shed blood to liberate have fallen one by one to ISIS, while Obama entertains transgenders at White House luncheons, and praises their courage. The Islamic extremists could blow up 20 American cities and he wouldn't say one unkind word about them. He would just mention some sort of generic "evil" without saying what specific evil we're dealing with.

I can't wait till he is out of office. Even Hillary Clinton would be tougher on Islamic terrorism than Obama, and I dread a Hillary Clinton presidency with all my heart.

MALO - 9.15

Mike Dukakis y George W. Bush hablaba español con fluidez. John Quincy Adams habla 7 idiomas con fluidez. James Garfield podría traducir Griego y Latín sin esfuerzo. Bueno para ellos.

In early September 2015 Donald Trump criticized Republican rival Jeb Bush for speaking Spanish on the campaign trail. Bush spoke Spanish to Spanish audiences of course, so what it your problemo, senor? Sure, it's good to have a national language, and yes, sometimes I get annoyed when I have to "choose a language" at the ATM, but don't make ignorance a virtue.

BIDEN HIS TIME

Vice President Joe Biden offended me in September 2015.

Now that Hillary Clinton's poll numbers are slipping, there is a groundswell of talk about VP Joe Biden maybe getting in the race. Biden is holding back before he makes a call. If Hillary holds on strong, he won't jump in. If she crashes in the polls he will. That's a pretty obvious dynamic at work here. I've no problem with that.

What really offends me is that Biden is answering questions about his potential candidacy by saying that it depends on whether he is emotionally capable of running. You see, it's all about the recent tragic death of his son. He has to consult with his family to see if they all could "handle" a run for president. After close consulting with his family he will soon decide. But it's all about whether he and his family are emotionally capable of it.

That's disgusting. Your son is dead either way. You have to go on living either way. You are emotionally capable of continuing on as the Vice President of the United States, no problem at all, but whether you declare your candidacy for president now supposedly depends on how you can go on after the death of your son.

What difference does it make? If it's so impossible to go on with life, no one is stopping you from resigning the Vice Presidency. Why not resign? Why is running for president so much more emotionally challenging than being the Vice President, supervising the Senate, traveling the world and making speeches to a thousand groups about a thousand subjects? My best friend died of cancer and it never crossed my mind to stop working. It's common knowledge that one of the best and most common ways for people to handle grief is to immerse themselves in work. What are Joe's plans? Is he going to cry 18 hours a day for the next 40 months and then go to sleep until he can wake up and start crying again?

Countless people have run for high office after a recent death in the family. The way the media is kissing his feet over his ostentatious grief issue really boils my cynical blood. Horace Greely ran for President while his wife was on her death bed. Franklin Pierce saw his son die before his own eyes in a train crash while he was president-elect. Woodrow Wilson lost his wife to the hereafter in August 1914. All of these people functioned well enough in the aftermath. Joe is a rich and famous politician. He has it easier than millions of people all over the world who lose a child to death and have to continue working while being poor.

Is Biden also fooling himself? Joe has managed to smile and take cheap shots at Republicans many times since his son died. All of a sudden he can't go on with life because of his grief, while he stumps for the Dems and continues on as VP. Joe Biden's decision to run for president depends on Hillary Clinton's poll numbers, not grief counseling consultations with his family.

"WHO'S EVEN HEARD OF LINDSEY GRAHAM?"

Donald Trump addressed a rally in early September by asking his audience, "Who is Lindsey Graham? Has anyone here ever heard of Lindsey Graham?" Laughter. Graham is criticizing Trump on the campaign trail.

After telling America for three months that he's never heard of Lindsey Graham, it no longer makes any sense. Of course you've heard of him; you've been saying his name as someone you've never heard of for far too long now, Don. Every time Lindsey Graham espouses a moderate Republican position, the right wing attacks him with cheap shots. Lindsey Graham is supposedly a RINO, a Republican in name only.

Lindsey Graham has been a United Senator from South Carolina since 1997. He led the Impeachment team of Republican Senators during the trial of Bill Clinton. He is a graduate of the University of South Carolina School of Law. He was in the United States Air Force, was a member of the House of Representatives and he was a candidate for President in 2012. I've heard of him, to answer your question, Mr. Trump. I don't pride myself on knowledge when it's convenient, and then on my ignorance when that's convenient.

Trump frustrates me because I want to vote for him in 2016, but his act, where he insults anyone who dares to criticize him, has lost its original refreshing novelty.

As of this writing in mid-September 2015 I am starting to leave the Trump camp and I'm drifting towards Carly Fiorina. At first I thought she was not viable, but she's looked very sharp in some recent interviews.

CARLY'S FACE

In mid September Donald Trump ridiculed the physical appearance of Carly Fiorina in a *Rolling Stone* interview:

"Look at that face! Would anyone vote for that? Can you imagine that, the face of our next president? I mean, she's a woman and I'm not supposed to say bad things, but really folks, come on, are we serious?"

That's it for me. I would vote for any candidate besides him. Trump had my vote for a couple of months but this is one Bostonian who will under no circumstances vote for Donald Trump. With all the talk in this country about how we must stop the bullying, along comes this thug and he expects to be the next president with this nonsense.

If I was Carly Fiorina's husband and I was lucky enough to be alone with Trump on an elevator, by the time he got off the elevator he'd be as cute as Abe Vigoda. What on earth does a candidate's looks have to do with whether they would make a good leader?

That's it. You're done, Don. I'll make an exception when he is in a national Presidential debate but that's it, you're done. I unfollowed Trump on social media and if he's doing a TV interview I watch a college basketball game instead. And I don't even follow college basketball.

THE SECOND REPUBLICAN DEBATE

Mid September: The 11 Republicans went at it again. The CNN moderator asked Carly Fiorina to address the comment Donald Trump had made about her face. She kept it short and said that all the women of America heard what he said loud and clear. She added that she didn't have to add anything. That got a round of applause. Donald Trump then jumped in and said that "Carly Fiorina is a beautiful woman and has a beautiful face." No one clapped. It was awkward because everyone could see what he was doing. He was trying to save face.

Now if someone wanted to poke fun at their own appearance playfully, that would have been different. Near the end, they asked each candidate what nickname they would like to have from the Secret Service if they were elected President. They started with Chris Christie who weighs about 350 pounds. He answered with something corny like "Braveheart." But if he had paused and said "fatso" the place would have erupted in an enormous laugh and cheer and he would have stolen the debate in one word. His comment would have been the lead story in every post-game show. - Jeb Bush scored here by ad-libbing, "Ever-ready, because like the battery, it has good energy." That got a huge laugh and applause because Trump had been criticizing Jeb Bush for having no energy, and it had been no doubt hurting Bush. Trump even smiled and gave Bush a sincere 'low-five' handshake.

THE FIRST DEMOCRATIC DEBATE

The Democrats finally hit the stage in Las Vegas with the first debate. It was Bernie Sanders and Hillary Clinton in the center. The three fringe candidates, off to the sides, were Martin O'Mally of Maryland, Jim Webb, the former governor of Virginia, and Lincoln Chaffee, the former RI senator and governor.

I thought all of the candidates did well, although Jim Webb let me down by complaining too much and too long about how he was not getting equal time. Don't waste 45 seconds moaning that you aren't getting the chance to get your message across. I agreed that Webb was getting shorted, but when you finally do get some time; don't give a long big baby speech about it. Dimwit.

I was surprised how much I liked Bernie Sanders, although he will have trouble getting Congress to help him realize his dramatic progressive rhetoric. He is so sincere! He is so New York. If it's him against Trump it will be a grouchy New York City lefty and a crusty New York City billionaire conservative. My wife and I agreed that Marty O'Malley did very well. MO was poised and articulate.

CNN did a horrible job producing this debate. Anderson Cooper is arrogant and egotistical, more of a prosecutor than a moderator, really. CNN treated the minutes leading into the debate like it was an NFL football game, with rock muzak, spinning images, instigator build-ups of who said what about who in the past, and a lot of other unspeakably gauche things. When Anderson Cooper was reading the rules, they actually had tense game show music in the background. I could barely hear what he was saying. It was a joke. They were trying to imitate the style of Who Wants to Be a Millionaire. I've never seen a debate produced this badly, and I've been taping and re-watching debates since 1983, the year I got my first VCR recorder.

KARL AND JOHN COME TO MANCHESTER

While doing a stand-up comedy gig in Manchester, New Hampshire, I accidentally stumbled into an insider Republican fundraiser and got to hear a keynote speech by Karl Rove. I also got the chance to say hello to candidate John Kasich, but I froze and let him walk by.

I was dressed up for my show so I sort of blended in. The room wasn't huge: 300 people. The entire time Karl Rove gave his speech there were two guys in suits up the back corner yapping to each other. You could hear them throughout the speech, no matter where you sat.

Take it outside you disgraceful vagabonds! How big do you have to get before people start showing proper respect?

The speech was about his latest book which is about the Election of 1896 and why it is still relevant. Dr. Ben Carson had been there earlier, but he'd left early. I went on stage in the adjoining, smaller room, 20 minutes after Rove finished up.

THIRD REPUBLICAN DEBATE

The third Republican debate took place in Boulder, Colorado. CNBC was the host. The wrestlers were Trump, Bush, Ted Cruz, Ben Carson, Mike Huckabee, Marco Rubio, John Kasich, and Chris Christie.

Fox News thought that Trump was the winner.

Only one or two R's have dropped out so far.

Jim Webb and Lincoln Chafee have dropped out for the Dems.

Highlight reels always pick the moments when people get mad at each other. In the case of Texas Senator Cruz, it was a matter of getting mad at the NBC moderators when he realized he couldn't bully them over the rules.

Bush and Rubio had it out over charges that Rubio was absent from his Senate desk too often in order to campaign for president. Bush repeated what he had been saying on the campaign trail: that Rubio should resign if he wants to campaign full time. Others have sought the presidency while still in Congress but they had better attendance records than Rubio.

Carly Fiorino pointed out that she had been criticized for not smiling enough during the last debate. So she smiled, without a word, for about 30 seconds. Carly is a better person than I am. When people lay that criticism on me, I yell at them.

F-35

Throughout 2015, the USA has begun to slowly deploy the first F-35 Lightning stealth fighters. They are to replace the F-16.

There are 1,800 of these fighter jets planned and the cost is $1.3 trillion, making it the highest priced conventional weapons system ever. Fortunately for the United States, many of its allies are picking up some of the tab.

SNL TRUMPED

Trump hosted *Saturday Night Live* on October 7, putting the leftist crew in a mixed message situation. The entire crew is 99% pro-Democrat (one guy that sweeps up the floor at the NBC commissary once voted for a Republican, but he denies it vehemently) yet they seem to like Trump. He was the host of the NBC series, *The Apprentice*; he's totally relaxed on camera; and he was a famous celebrity in America for decades. So Trump came out, embraced his negatives humorously, defused them, and did a very good job as comedy host.

Not that I think anyone can beat Hillary in 2016, but Trump sure did himself a favor with his evening on SNL. He put them in a box where they couldn't live up to my nickname for them: Saturday Night Left.

SNL is now in a position where they will not be able to put a torpedo into Trump like they did to Bush and McCain and every other previous R-candidate, going back to Gerald Ford. Chevy Chase openly admitted in past interviews that the SNL crew was trying to take Ford down and help elect Jimmy Carter, and they did. But now they can only playfully make fun of Trump from here on in, which they will of course. But now their bark is worse than their bite, which wasn't the case in the past. The NBC link defuses SNL's stick of dyn-o-myte.

Hillary Clinton did well last month when she was on SNL, but Trump did better, and Hillary already had SNL in her corner before she went on. She didn't gain all that much. But Trump has turned one of the most vicious opponents every Republican president has to overcome, *Saturday Night Live*, and rendered it relatively harmless, almost benevolent. I said almost. Seeing all these lefties hugging and chatting with Trump over the closing credits was most interesting. He forced them all to take the firing pin out of their very deadly guns.

As of this writing, November 8, 2015, I don't like anyone for President. If it's Hillary vs. Trump, I have no idea what to do, and it probably will be.

PARIS TERROR ATTACKS - 11.13.15

They are calling themselves ISIL now; more often than ISIS. On the night of November 11, ISIL struck at several soft targets in and around Paris. They killed 130 innocent civilians watching sports, listening to a music concert and sipping coffee in cafes.

SAN BERNARDINO ATTACKS

This one had the nation in a 3-day panic. A young married Muslim couple went berserk on 12.2.15 and killed 14 people. Why? For absolutely no reason at all. It happened in San Bernardino, California, at a social services center, of all places.

DECEMBER 12 - REPUBLICAN DEBATE

They held it in the Venetian Hotel showroom in Las Vegas, probably so Chris Christie could go play craps and place sports bets at the nearby Hilton. CNN hosted, and Wolf Blitzer did a much better job keeping his ego out of it than Anderson Cooper did in the last one I saw. I've missed a few debates, I've seen a few, and there's plenty to go.

The one thing that stood out for me was how strong Ted Cruz looked. I've disliked him rather strongly up to this point, but a few nights ago I saw something I hadn't seen before. I saw real strength, especially debating strength. He's too far to the right for me, especially on religion, so I'd be less than thrilled if he's the guy, but Trump is a fool, and Jeb is never going to catch fire.

The big moment of the debate was when Jeb got tough and said to Trump, "Donald, you cannot simply insult your way to the presidency." Unfortunately he apparently can insult his way to the nomination. And Trump rolled his eyes and said sarcastically, "Oh yeah, Jeb, you're a real tough guy." The schoolyard bully thing hurts both candidates for me. It scores against Bush because it happened, however unfairly and mean; and it scores against Trump as a really bad person.

PHILLY COP ATTACK

On January 7, 2016, a black man in Philly ran up to a police car that was stopped at a red light and shot the driver. The wounded cop opened the door and gave chase to the fleeing gunman.

They caught the guy. The shooter was a Muslim and he did it for ISIS, did it for Islam, did it for Allah, and did not regret it. Obviously a religious hate crime right? Right.

The Mayor of Philadelphia gets on TV and tells the nation that this attack "in no way had anything to do with Islam." His own police chief had earlier said it did, but the chief was now changing his tune too. It had nothing at all to do with Islam.

The shooter said he did it for Islam.

Tomorrow 95% of the social media people will be furious, not at the guy who shot the cop, but at the right wing reactionaries who think this had anything to do with Islam! The liberals in America ridicule all religions except Islam. Go figure. The most illiberal religion on earth, and that's the ones the liberals defend.

2016 - REPUBLICAN JANUARY 16 DEBATE

Debate Party tonite: Break out the nuts, and watch them. Once again I thought Ted Cruz did well, and bested Trump in their little spats.

As usual Ben Carson, the Republican black guy, was atrocious, Chris Christie was all histrionics, Jeb Bush was good but not good enough, Kasich did well but no one cares, and everyone acted like a baby because they weren't called on enough.

Cruz got Trump all riled up by playing the New York City Card. I think it worked well for Cruz and Trump fell for the bait. Cruz had made a statement that Trump represented "New York values." The Fox immoderator asked Cruz and Trump to talk about that, and sparks flew.

I've been saying the same thing about Trump all along, and not in a bad way. The guy is from New York City. He can pretend to be a redneck all he wants, but the guy is from New York City. Right wing Republicans claim that Trump is way more liberal than he wants you to realize, and it makes him more attractive to a national electorate. He needs to play right wing nut in order to lock down the Republican nomination. A more moderate Trump would likely emerge after he wins the nomination. If he does.

Cruz is mean and very capable. He kept his cool while Trump got angry. Instead of addressing the city-slicker charge, Trump launched into a cornball account of the 911 WTC tragedy, complete with valueless irrelevant points about the fortitude and quality of New York City people.

Cruz stuck to his guns and said, "Not a lot of conservatives come out of Manhattan. I'll just leave it at that."

The point is dead on. I couldn't agree more. No one can be from Manhattan and end up a Ted Cruz conservative. He's got Trump on this point.

Cruz knows that New York State will not vote Republican in 2016. It's a lock for the Dems, and Manhattan votes almost 90% Democrat. So Cruz has nothing to lose by making New Yorkers furious with him. And Trump took the bait, thinks there's nothing to the charge, and thinks that telling a Giullianiesque 911 story will change the subject and save him here. But it doesn't. A day later Trump is appealing to his New York City fan base and ripping Cruz. The headlines in the NY papers are Trump telling Cruz off and saying "If You Don't Like My New York Values, Go Back to Canada."

Bush the First did it to Dukakis in 1988 when he ripped Massachusetts, ripped Boston Harbor, ripped New England liberalism and left me wondering how I could support this guy after he tears my home state to shreds. But that was the same strategy. We aren't going to win Massachusetts anyway, so let's reverse 'turn' it. Take a potential asset and turn it into a deliberate liability. Clever and effective.

Can Cruz beat Trump? The poll numbers are about 35% Trump, 15% Cruz and the rest divided. So it's 2-1 Trump and he's had the big lead for months.

What is going to happen when the other Republicans drop out? Are their supporters going to go to Cruz, or to Trump? Everyone pretty much either loves or hates Trump right now. He has a strong lead and his campaign is still holding back on money. If he starts to fall he can throw a billion bucks into the race at the 11th hour. So he is going to be tough to stop, no matter what. But I see Cruz picking up momentum as it goes along and making it close by the summer. The more Trump has to drop the insult act and act presidential, the more this plays to the advantage of Cruz, who I think is the only one in the field who can beat Hillary Clinton in a debate. I think Hillary can beat Trump in a debate, period. He is more vulnerable as he rises. Granted, Trump's supporters are not, repeat, not going to desert him. But he has to find some new supporters if he is to continue on course and I feel that he has no new fields to plow and harvest there, and Cruz does.

I am absolutely positively undecided. I would not rule out voting for either Donald Trump or Hillary Clinton. I neither love, nor hate either one of them which leaves me of course with no friends. I like all four front runners just enough to consider them all, now that Ben Carson is no longer in the top four. And if there is anything I am looking forward to, it's the day Ben Carson drops out of the race and I never have to listen to him again. Cruz is way too far to the right for me! But I have come to really respect his skills set. I thought he destroyed Rubio, the most miserable man alive for some strange reason, by keeping cool and letting his words do the talking, whereas Rubio relies on faces and tones (all miserable) to make his points.

A year ago I made a study of the United States Senate and made a slide show of all 100 of them. About four or five Senators really impressed me with the clear fact that they are potential Supreme Court nominees. Michael Bennet in Colorado was one, and Ted Cruz was another. I remember the Canada thing too and wondered through the second half of 2015 when that was finally going to come up as an issue in his run for President.

So when Trump went after Cruz for being supposedly unqualified to run for President; and Cruz said that he was not going to be lectured on the law by Donald Trump, I nodded along approvingly.

Trump has great assets as a business person and he brings that major quality to the table. But on foreign affairs he is learning as you go, and that's not good. Hillary Clinton does have a major advantage in having been Secretary of State. Even the Hil-haters might have to concede that this experience is at least reassuring that there will be no dramatic great blunder in the transitional year.

IOWA CAUCUSES - 2.1.16

Finally, after two years of listening to the windbags, some actual voting begins. Ted Cruz pulled off a big upset win over favorite Donald Chump, and Father Rubio finished a close third. (Cruz 30% - Trump 24% - Father Rubio 23%.)

I call him Father Rubio because the Florida "Senator" is playing the 'Jesus Christ is My Lord and Savior' card to the hilt, and it has worked for him. I will never vote for him ever, because this offends me. You aren't acting like Christ, but you're invoking him officially, to pander for votes. You're a bad boy.

On the Democratic side, Bernie Sanders had a great night, losing to heavy favorite Hillary Clinton by a microscopic two-tenths of one percent! No one had been predicting anything that close.

Part of Hillary's problem are strong rumors that the Federal Bureau of Investigation may indict her for breaches of national security regarding her careless sending of classified material over her private e-mail account.

Personally, I don't resent this matter enough to make it decide my vote. I know it wasn't deliberate, and that it won't happen again. Mrs. Clinton is very experienced on foreign policy and I might prefer to have someone manage foreign policy that I do not agree with, with great efficiency, as opposed to someone managing a policy I agree with, with great inefficiency.

If the Clintons had not made enemies out of the FBI during their time in power in the 90's, the FBI would not be proceeding with indictments. It looks 60-40 to me like it's going to happen.

Then what? Bernie Sanders, a man slightly to the left of Howard Zinn becomes president. No way is that a good thing and I actually hope Hillary does not get indicted.

RUBIO ROBOT - 2.6.16

Florida Senator Marco Rubio came into the GOP NH Debate at St. Anselm College as the hottest candidate in the race on either side. But Governor Chris Christie made him look foolish in a harsh exchange at around the 15 minute mark.

I had not seen the debate live, but the word was so out that Rubio had tanked that I looked it up on the internet to judge for myself. Often you read about someone winning or losing a debate that you saw and ask, "Did this person see the same debate that I saw?" The Boston Herald headlined a picture of his face with the word CHOKE! as the headline! This I gotta see.

Sure enough, the headline and the reaction were fair and just. Marco Rubio, my least favorite of the serious candidates, did indeed melt down.

Christie and Rubio were arguing about something very specific and Rubio switched into the robot act. He went into a speech about how Obama has ruined this country, and when he becomes President, he will do this and do that. It was all rhetoric, exactly like one would hear at one of his campaign rallies. I'm getting sick of the slick robot speeches from him with no substance. His only platform is that Obama has ruined this country and he will fix what Obama has broken. He doesn't say how, but he says he will. Anyway, it was so out of context that Christie went after him on this very point, telling Rubio that all he ever does is launch into rehearsed 25 second speeches, and how everyone is getting tired of it. The crowd was all abuzz. But what really made Rubio look bad was how he made a token counter-attack at Christie and then, inexplicably, launched the same standard campaign speech, repeating the same lines he had just used a few minutes ago, while the crowd was all upset, booing, hissing, laughing; and meanwhile Christie is shaking his head in disbelief telling the camera, "See what I mean? Just vague rhetoric, all rehearsed." Rubio droned on and on while the whole world saw him as a fool, his staunch supporters excepted of course.

In four minutes, Christie shook up the order of the Republicans trying to catch up to Trump (who had a good night.)

CHRIS CHRISTIE DROPS OUT

I'll say two positive things first. Christie had some great moments in the debates. Not just good. Great. You could see he has talent, and he made some great points. CC was well-spoken on some subjects. Also, he set an all-American standard for going after what you want. He ran for the presidency with 110% effort.

But clearly he is a bully. If I had to be in a room and disagree with him on something, he would just launch into a tirade against me an inch from my nose, until I would have to flee the room. I'm not easily intimidated, but I'd meet my match with Christie. Even more than Trump! Trump is a bully, but you might score a point which could make Trump break down and maybe even smile, but Christie wants to hurt you in a debate and that is the beginning and the end of it. The playing of the WTC card was very offensive to me. One time, okay, but over and over? Terrible. What year is this? And even though he did have his moments, most of the time you just pray for the moment when he will just shut his pie-hole and give your frazzled brain a rest. The playing to the camera instead of the moderator or the studio audience was awkward, and did not work. But the one thing that offended me the most was his relentless false point that being a governor is so much tougher than being a senator.

The office of senator is more powerful than that of governor. How many ex-senators are now governors? How many ex-governors are now senators? At least a dozen for the latter, maybe one of the former. - Senators have to make decisions about sending Americans to fight and die in combat. Governors do not. They are both demanding jobs, but he never let up on how being a senator is nothing compared to the tough decisions one has to make as governor. Really offensive and not based on reality except in his mind, and even then, I doubt if he really believed that.

When he first started running for president, all I could think of was, "Every single person I know from New Jersey can't stand this guy! How is he supposed to use his track record as governor to run for President?" He shuffled the facts and focused on contrived points, and he raised his voice.

He did the right thing for everyone and made his thug side useful for once, when he exposed Rubio for the lame rhetoric machine that he is. When Chris Christie is repulsed by your shallow rhetoric, you know you're in trouble!

GILMORE OUT

Ex-Virginia Governor Jim Gilmore dropped out of the Republican race on February 11, the same day as the PBS softball debate between Hillary Clinton and Bernie Sanders. I watched it with my wife and we both thought Hillary won, and not because my wife's name is Hilarie. We are both undecided voters and she never tells me who she votes for and I never ask. I still have her vote for husband and that's a crucial swing vote I depend on.

Bernie Sanders is 74 and he coughs his way through the debates. If a Republican was doing that, the TV shows would be making montages and endless jokes about it.

I was very offended by what Sanders said about Kissinger and Cambodia. He blames the United States for the Killing Fields, and that is not fair, accurate, or true.

He says that the American incursion into Cambodia during the Vietnam War destabilized that country, brought about the downfall of Sinahouk, and led to the Killing Fields.

No. Cambodia was already destabilized and was in the process of falling to the Red Communists - and the Killing Fields was what happened and what was going to happen as soon as AMERICA LEFT THE REGION, not because it was there.

TONY SCALIA - 2.13.16

The Supreme Court suffered a sudden death in the nine member family on February 13, 2016, when Justice Antonin Scalia went to meet the supreme judge. At 79, Scalia was the oldest member of the court, and the most conservative. The Reagan appointee died in his sleep while away on a quail-hunting trip to Texas.

FEBRUARY 13 R DEBATE - SUPREME COURT INJUSTICE

I take back what I said earlier about Rubio the robot. He had a good debate, and showed some courage in defending the record of G. W. Bush. I will reconsider him for my vote.

Donald Trump had his worst debate. Not that it will hurt his ratings. Nothing apparently can. He was rude and immature toward everyone. He interrupted, acted like a baby, and managed to bring the tone down to the gutter all night. Yet it will not hurt him, for those who love him already know that he is like that. It's too bad because I liked him for a while, then he lost me, then he started to win me back a little (I thought his last debate was his best and when he talked about making sure there were no more homeless on the street, I thought he came through as really sincere and that, who knows, maybe he will do something about this) and then last night he was at his worst.

He called Ted Cruz a liar and a "nasty person."

Why?

Because Cruz had accurately reminded Trump that he had defended federal funding for Planned Parenthood. Trump became furious and called Cruz a liar. Cruz said that 'You certainly did say that early on in the campaign' and then Trump interrupted, interrupted and interrupted. It was infantile.

Don, I was watching that night when O'Reilly interviewed you while the people in the background were riding up the escalator and waving. You stuck to your guns and said you would not cut federal funding for Planned Parenthood because they do a lot of other great things. I liked you for it. There was no discussion of separating the money into two accounts, one for abortions, and one for everything else. That has never been an option. It was all or nothing, and when pressed, you showed courage and bucked the Party. Break out the tapes folks. Ted

Cruz was dead on. Trump did say that in New York City on Fox. O'Reilly couldn't, or wouldn't press him on it. Bill actually deferred.

So when Ted Cruz sees an opportunity to put him on the spot in ultraconservative South Carolina five months later, Trump's only response is "You're a liar! You're even a bigger liar than Jeb Bush! You're a nasty guy. You are really a nasty guy. No wonder no one likes you."

Cruz "Donald, that's not very mature."

Trump; "Oh yeah, like you're mature."

That's really close to verbatim.

Also, Don, I don't like your slogan, "Let's Make America Great Again."

So it's not a great country now?

Why? Because you aren't in charge? Because a liberal is in charge? I happen to think that America is a great country, period. Plus you stole the slogan from the Reagan campaign of 1980.

Falsehood #3 - "If it weren't for me, no one would even be talking about illegal immigration." - Immigration has been a hot button topic for about the last 25 years and it is always brought up during the presidential debates. For the last decade it has been a really controversial and prominent national debate subject. Don, if you had never been born, it would have been brought up during the 2016 debates.

But if it's you against Sanders, I will campaign for you, pal. Trump will be my main man! On the other hand, if it's you against Hillary Clinton, I will probably (but not definitely) vote for a Democrat for president for the first time in my life. I like the fact that she doesn't hate Wall Street the way Sanders does, and that she is a hawk compared to him.

As for Justice Scalia, some of the vicious things that have been said about him while his body lay unburied are shameful.

Meanwhile, the attempt of the Republicans to block *any* appointment to the Supreme Court is red-alert unjust. Obama and the Democrats won the Election fair and square, and Mr. Obama should be able to name the next Justice.

And don't tell me about what the Dems once did to Judge Bork etc. If the Democrats do the same, I'll condemn them too.

The Democratic Party this summer could put a plank in the platform that in the future the D Party will not follow the Republican example, and that the party is pledged to work with any sitting President to confirm a Supreme Court nominee during that president's tenure. If the Republicans get away with this, let it be the last time it ever happens.

Where does one draw the line? 10 months, fifteen months, three years? Taken to its logical extreme, an obstructionist Congress could prevent a Supreme Court nominee from confirmation for four years, or even 8. There might eventually be one 99 year old guy left on the Court, because Mitch McConnell thinks the country will be better off without liberal justices.

This obstructionism is not in the spirit of the Constitution or of democracy. This sets a terrible precedent. I guess it's time to switch back to Independent.

If the Dems win in November, the Republicans might refuse to act on a new justice until Hillary is voted out in 2020.

So the R's want to make the November election about Roe v. Wade. Lot's O' Luck! Your best road to the White House is to focus on foreign policy and peace through strength, not division through obstruction.

Ohio Governor John Kasich might be good for me, but it's hard to start a fire for someone who can't start one on his own. But he is growing on me. Carson makes some great short speeches on occasion, but he also says some of the most cringe-worthy statements ever uttered.

Every time Trump has it out with someone, someone else says that 'We all have to stop this bickering and stand united to defeat the Democrats,' yet no one will come out and mention that it's Trump in the middle of it, 95% of the time.

I thought Hillary Clinton defeated Sanders soundly in their last debate. If Jeb Bush didn't stammer on every other sentence, he would be doing much better. Trump might be making a mistake making the Bush machine hate him. If and when Bush drops out, there's a lot of juice that is going to someone else, and it won't be Trump.

TRUMP SETS A NEW LOW IN PRESIDENTIAL CAMPAIGNING

Trump couldn't take it when Cruz pointed out some true facts, and, as we have seen, went ballistic on Cruz during the 2/13 debate.

So the next day Trump calls a press conference to announce that he is suing Ted Cruz as being ineligible to run for President because he is a liar and is mentally unstable! The blind hypocrite is going to sue the one person he discovered he couldn't verbally bully. Then his document goes on to say that he is going to sue Cruz as being ineligible to run for President because he was born in Canada. There's at least an argument there – not a very strong one – but at least one is there. The Constitution is vague on this matter, like it is on too many things, but at least it's a legal issue. Trump suing Cruz for being mentally unstable makes me think that Trump is mentally unstable. Trump's behavior during the last debate was the most mentally unbalanced performance in the history of Presidential debates. No one has ever acted like that before.

On the night of the 14th I saw a bulletin that Trump is feuding with the RNC, claiming that it is treating him unfairly. I should have posted what I was thinking: "This is a set up for him to break his pledge to stick with the Republicans no matter what."

He pledged without condition, a couple of months ago, to not run as a third party candidate if he does not get the R-nomination. Now he is trying to blackmail the Republican Party. He says that if the RNC doesn't start treating him better he will not only withdraw from the Party, he will sue Ted Cruz on the Canada issue. Apples and oranges blackmail is loony.

Donald Trump is the most dangerous demagogue to ever run for president and stands as the front runner at this late stage of the game. He makes Huey Long look like a piker. Trump could easily start WWIII with the Russians by inflaming an international crisis with his insufferable lunatic ego. People hate his guts all over the world right now, and he is the most hated man in the United States of America. If he wins, he will be 10 times more hated than any president in US history. To those who like him, I ask the question, do you think that will be good for America? I remember when he was my guy, I used to think that the way people hated him would be bad for the country. I was therefore hesitant to hope that he wins, even though I liked him.

Donald is making Cruz and Rubio look like moderates, which they are not. In a way he is helping them win some center support, like with me. If Trump behaved like a decent person instead of a bully, thug, sick-in-the-head egomaniac with the maturity of a six-year-old, I might embrace him and his POV on quite a few issues and I would not like Cruz or Rubio at all! But in this case DT's individual personality is the problem, not his policies.

As for the Dems, they are setting themselves up for the Goldwater syndrome with Bernie Sanders. In 1964 the Republicans wanted anyone but Goldwater. They knew that Barry Goldwater was too extreme to win a general election, but also had to deal with the fact that as a hard rightist, Goldwater could, and did, roll up the right and win the nomination. The Republican leadership watched in horror as Goldwater's grass roots conservative campaign succeeded; and they watched helplessly as LBJ knocked him senseless in the general election. Sanders is rolling up the hard left, and if/when he gets into the general election he should get clobbered. If it's Trump vs. Sanders I might have to just not vote. That would be a nightmare.

BUSHWHACKED

Jeb Bush, as of February 16, has now dropped from 12% to about 4% in the national polls. It's time for him to drop out. Trump, the schoolyard bully, has beaten him up, and Jeb is toast. Trump has even gone so far as to blame George W. Bush for the fall of the World Trade Center Towers. That's the first time I ever heard anyone say that! It happened on W's watch, so he obviously "failed to keep us safe." Trump hates everyone and everything except himself. Some people tell me that the real problem is that he hates himself.

Meanwhile, Dr. Ben Carson made a fool of himself, as usual, by saying that the Founding Fathers only agreed to a lifetime tenure for Supreme Court nominees because "the average life expectancy at the time was less than 50 years of age." That is not true. Most Founding Fathers lived long happy lives. What a foolish thing to say. Carson has ruined the expression "You don't have be a brain surgeon to know that." Carson rewrites the expression to mean "Heck, even a brain surgeon can figure that one out!"

WALL

Trump says repeatedly that he is going to build a wall between Mexico and America to keep the illegal invaders out. He also says he is going to deport each and every illegal immigrant, and only when they are all out will he decide which ones to even consider letting back in. This would involve millions of people being arrested and shipped to Mexico. Yeah, that'll go as smooth as one of your made-in-China silk ties.

So many people really love him for both of these ideas, and so many people hate him for these ideas. I see both sides as having some merit, but I clearly side against Trump. Illegal immigration invasion is serious, but the USA doesn't want to behave in a cruel manner about anything if any alternative is available. Both of these ideas are just too mean.

For a while people challenged him about how expensive it would be to build a Great Wall of the USA. He says now that he will make Mexico pay for it, thus fending off the most obvious real problem with an unreal solution.

How cruel such a wall would look from a satellite-cam. There's that big mean country with its big mean wall. Half a million full time new border patrol guards would provide as much deterrence as a 40 billion dollar wall. Even if a wall worked, the immigrants will just find some other way to get in here. It would disperse them to varied routes and schemes, but they'd still get here. If the nation builds a 40 billion dollar wall and it ends up doing little or nothing to stop the flow of illegal immigrants, imagine how bad that will be in so many ways.

VIVA LA PAPA!

Pope Francis made a statement today that swept the globe. He said that Donald Trump is not a real Christian if he keeps talking about building walls to keep people out.

Trump responded by saying he's going to slap the Pope the next time he sees him. Okay, I'm exaggerating, but Don was pretty bold in saying that the Pope has no right to judge him. Trump said that the Pope obviously doesn't have enough information on the issues, and suggested some Papa hypocrisy by pointing out that there are walls around the Vatican.

Duh!

As if a 400 year old benevolent wall in a tiny area of free-roaming tourists around the Vatican has any relation to building a hate-wall across the giant US-Mexico border. In any case, the wall idea doesn't bother me as much as his idea of rounding up 12 million illegals living in America and deporting them. That's a river of tears. I just hope the Pope can put a grease slick on Trump's apparently unstoppable road to the nomination.

NOT SINCE MEDIEVAL TIMES?

If I had a dollar for every inaccurate statement Trump makes, I'd buy a Ferrari. One he keeps repeating is:

"You have ISIS cutting people's heads off and lighting people on fire! That hasn't happened since medieval times!"

I've heard it a dozen times. Hideous executions have not taken place like this "since Medieval times." You drip. The Nazi Holocaust? The Rape of Nanking? Rwanda? Liberia? Cambodia? Armenia? Lenin's Red Terror? The Philippine Insurrection? And that's only a fast take on the 20th Century. The French Revolution took place long after "Medieval times."

The other day he actually defended Iraqi dictator Sadaam Hussein, saying that "He made a living killing terrorists." Most Trump supporters even had to admit that this was absurd, and completely out of line. Trump praised an enemy of the United States who had killed American soldiers and airmen. Yet his fans never reach a point where they desert him. He is the worst charlatan of all time; a monster. He gets his facts totally wrong over and over but asserts them so brazenly, with so much confidence that he gets away with it.

As for that coughing machine Bernie Sanders, he's doing great with his slogan "Feel the Bern." Yeah, you will all feel the economy Bern the day he takes over as the avowed inveterate enemy of free enterprise and capitalism.

BUSH BURNED OUT

Jeb Bush suspended his campaign or the Presidency on February 20, 2016. Why do they all use that euphemism? Like that isn't "ending" your campaign. That's like a man at home telling his wife, "My job at the coal mine has been suspended." - "You mean you got fired?" - "Yes."

Trump, who bullied Bush mercilessly during the debates, said today, "Bush ran a good campaign, it just wasn't his time. He's a very capable guy." Hey Don, you blow.

CARSON IS HILARIOUS

After Jeb Bush dropped out, there was speculation that Ben Carson should drop out, too. His response:

"I am not going anywhere."

Truer words have never been spoken.

Doc Ben Carson started out the debate with a really fine and crucial point, and then it was all downhill from there. Dickenson of ABC (a really excellent moderator) asked him, pursuant to the vacant seat on the Supreme Court: "What does the Constitution say about whose duty it is to act in this kind of a situation?"

Carson: "Well the Constitution doesn't actually address that particular situation."

Yes indeed! - Big C is a highly imperfect document, and it is time to amend it to make some rules about "that particular situation."

Then Ben says this:

"But the fact the matter is, the Supreme Court is obviously a very important part of our governmental system, and when our Constitution was put in place, the average age of death, was under 50, and therefore the whole concept of lifetime appointments for Supreme Court judges and Federal judges, was not considered to be a big deal. Obviously that has changed. And it's something that ah probably needs to be looked at pretty carefully at some point."

This false point again about the age of the Founders had me shaking my head. How many times can he say silly things and stay in the race? I have studied the Constitution "pretty carefully" and I can assure you that this concern about lack of longevity was not part of the thinking in 1787, even if it were true about the under 50 span. Lifetime tenure is lifetime tenure, whether it's 40 or 79. What difference would that make in the system?

And what changes exactly do you have in mind after it's looked at pretty carefully. If a Supreme Court Justice becomes so old and feeble as to border insanity, they can be removed by an impeachment process; and that *is* in the Constitution, so what's your issue here between 49 and 79?

The lifetime tenure is in there to protect the other two branches from imposing its will on the court. It has nothing to do with the lifespan of judges in 1787.

I knew that this lifespan thing was not accurate. But I didn't want to lose three hours of work confirming something that I already knew: that the lifespan of the men of 1787 was not less than 50 years of age, even factoring in deaths at birth. So I asked my friend, comedian and history student Johnny Pizzi, if he would make a list of the 39 signers of the Constitution and list their age upon death. He did it, and clearly the average age of death is well into the 60's.

Here's Doc's answer to a question by John Dickerson about casualties in Iraq and whether they are acceptable. (And stammering counts! It means you aren't square shouldered confident.)

Carson: *"Well first of all, let me just, ah, address the Iraq question. You know, I was not particularly in favor of ah, us going to war in Iraq,* [so? you were a doctor with a personal opinion - big deal, and even now you equivocate with 'particularly'] *primarily ah I've fffsssss studied, you know, the Middle East, recognizing that those are nations that are ruled by dictators, and have been for thousands of years* [I roared laughing at this one - thousands of years? - Grow a brain cell, brain surgeon. Nationhood is a relatively new concept! He seems unsure of himself most of the time. Pathetic, really. I might have seen few open-mikers with less speaking confidence. He's so awful. Once in a while he gets on a well-trained point and gets his applause, but it's never in direct relation to the original question.] ... *In terms of the rules of engagement, I was talking about, you know, Obama has said, you know, we shouldn't bomb tankers, eh you know coming out of refineries, cause there may be* <u>people</u> *in there, or because the environment may be hurt. You know, that's just asinine thinking, [applause] and the fact of the matter is, you know we ah obviously you're not going to accomplish all of your goals without some collateral damage. You have to assess what is acceptable and what is not."*

He actually said the last sentence without stammering! What tankers are you talking about? What news story am I missing here? This is as disjointed in print as anything two paragraphs in my library. The USA is not at war with Iran and is trying to build a positive relation with Iran, whether you agree with it or not. What tankers are you recommending that your country smash up, killing people and creating a huge oil slick? What on earth are you talking about? When are you going to GO AWAY, and let real candidates have the floor? And stop complaining throughout every debate that you aren't being asked enough questions. You're last in all the polls and that's the way it works.

And thanks for the bloodthirsty take on collateral damage, Mr. Christian.

Moderate moderator Dickinson then asked him to say one thing that might be unpopular to say but people need to know.

Ben starts out with the irrelevant cheap point that having no experience is an asset, but even then he messes up this old canard:

"Well first of all, I'm not a politician, and I'm never going to become one."

Ha ha ha ha! Ben Carson, you're even funnier than Johnny Carson! The day you become President you are of course a politician.

And here's the first part of his closing statement:

"This is the first generation not expected to do better than their parents [based on what? I hear this every four years, so how can this be the first one?]. *Some people say, it's the new normal. There's nothing normal about it, in an exceptional America. I, like you, am a member of 'we, the people,' and we know that our country is heading off the cliff. Joseph Stalin said, 'If you want to bring America down, you have to undermine three things, our spiritual life, our patriotism, and our morality.'*

Maybe Stalin said this. I am most definitely a Stalin scholar and I have never heard Joe say anything like that. It doesn't sound like him at all. He was a practical & ruthless man, not a philosopher. That sounds like someone else. I'd love to know the source of that one.

Will you please drop out, Ben Carson? Do the right thing. You have no chance. At least Bush showed some fortitude in facing reality. He didn't need the media attention as an ego ride. But you are just enjoying all the media attention, and being selfish. You have as much chance as a bee in a blizzard.

TRUMP ANCESTRY

You learn something new every day! Now I find out that Donald Trump's grandfather made his fortune running whore houses in the Pacific Northwest, and that Donald's dad, Fred, was evidently a member of the Ku Klux Klan, who was also successfully prosecuted by the FBI for racial discrimination in New York City.

Fred Trump was arrested at a Klan rally in 1923 after the hoods scuffled with the police. There is no proof that that he was a Klansman, but he was bailed out of jail by a Klan lawyer.

Trump's defense when shown the police records and newspaper accounts? "That never happened."

THE HANDICAPPED REPORTER

Today I also found out about an incident last November that I somehow missed: Trump mocked a physically challenged reporter. *The New York Times* reporter had exposed Trump as a liar when Trump said that thousands of Muslims in New Jersey had danced in the streets celebrating the fall of the World Trade Center Towers. That had not happened. Trump's response was to demand an apology and to mock the reporter's disability with a pantomime. It was one of the most sickening things I have ever seen in my life and when I saw it, I had to post it on Facebook with the following comment:

Somehow I missed this one. I know it's old news, but it's new to me. Trump is over the top mocking a person with a physical disability; and because that reporter caught him in a proven lie! Literally sickening to me. And in response he demands an apology from the reporter! Any policeman, schoolteacher or even office worker caught doing this would be immediately suspended without pay pending further action, or fired. And he might be my president! I didn't vote for Obama but I feel he has a good heart, and I hope he is correct, that the American people will not make this man President, but I don't know. No matter what he does, people still adore him. Good God almighty have mercy on our poor country if he gets in. Can you watch this and still stand by him? This is the worst thing I have ever seen in a public figure. Evil. Stand up comics aren't this cruel in a late show Friday dive gig. So wrong. - "Appears to mock?" - This man always has total control of his hand and arm gestures. He knew exactly what he was doing. - This made me cry."

LAST R DEBATE BEFORE SUPER-TUESDAY

Marco Rubio had an excellent debate and ripped into Trump, shaking the superjerk up for the first time. Pundits on all sides agreed that someone finally put a dent into Trump but most also said it's too late to stop him.

So the other superjerk, New Jersey thug governor Chris Christie comes out the next morning and endorses Trump who he hammered during the debate as someone completely unqualified to be President. Christie deliberately timed it to take the momentum away from Rubio, and it worked. All everyone is talking about now is Christie endorsing Trump. They held a press conference and practically made out with each other. The idea of a Trump-Christie ticket brings two words to mind: Totalitarian government.

Ben Carson made a fool of himself as usual. Kasich is the big loser with the Christie endorsement because obviously he is afraid to criticize Trump because he's angling for the VP spot.[1] Kasich is much more of a redneck than Joe Public realizes. His past record (a TV show ran clips to prove) show him as a grouchy rightie hard-liner.

I'm disappointed with the media for not making the lead story Trump's rudeness. That is the lead. I am a Republican who plans to switch to the Democratic Party if this monster wins. He says nothing productive, and insults everyone. He said recently that he could murder someone and he would not lose any support. That is true. So

---

[1] I strongly disagree with me on this, looking back from 2018. Kasich was never angling to be Trump's VP. Kasich was the best.

what does that tell you about his support? He is a fascist. I pray for my country if he wins. He is an evil man who obviously does not even believe in God. The same way Obama got out the vote in 2008, all decent people in America need to get every other decent person in America to register to vote him down in November. There's no stopping him from winning the Republican nomination. He mocks the handicapped and you fans are okay with that? What happened to the national campaign against bullying? It applies to children, but it's okay for adults?

"Make America Hate Again."

DAVID DUKE ENDORSES TRUMP - PERFECT!

Former Ku Klux Klan leader David Duke endorsed Donald J. Trump for president, followed by a few statements why. I'd rather not quote them.

A day or two later, on CNN, Trump was confronted by a TV host over whether he would reject Duke's support. Trump repeatedly said, "I've never heard of David Duke, so how can I reject his support?" Plain as day he said it over and over. When asked if he would reject the support of white supremacists, Trump kept saying he didn't know what that meant, so he obviously couldn't comment on it. "I've never heard of a white supremacist, I don't know what that is, so obviously I can't comment on it."

For the next 48 hours the media, and all decent people, made the most of this vicious refusal to denounce the support of a racist kingpin. The thing snowballed until on February 29, Trump took a leap backwards, a rare event, and claimed that a "bad earpiece" during the interview caused him to not realize what he was being asked. Then he said, "of course" he rejected the support of David Duke. It had been hardly a matter of course to get this out of Trump.

David Duke has been a famous name in America for decades. I saw the original interview and Trump clearly knew what he was being asked and just lied, and claimed he had never heard of David Duke or white supremacists, just so he could avoid rejecting their endorsement.

Many Republican and religious leaders are denouncing Trump in every way possible public way, but his support does not waver. I never knew how many devil-loving racist rednecks there really were in this country until now. I will gladly lose friends over this man.

Republican Senate leader Mitch McConnell is calling on all Republican candidates to run attack ads on their own front-runner for President! Holy Mackerel! The GOP is leading the calls to action to stop this dictator! Every day millions are posting well articulated essays on why he is wrong and must be stopped, and all his supporters can write back is, "F___ you loser! Trump in 2016! You are finally going to see a real man in the White House!"

Trump haters attack intelligently, and at length: Trump defenders fight back with short stupid sentences of thug-think. The pattern is clear; dumb racist rednecks are supporting him and the rest of the country (and the world) is against him. It is the worst nightmare ever! I never hated anyone or anything more. And hating evil is not hate! It's anger in the name of love and decency!

Religious leaders all over the country are urging their flock to leave Trump. Millions of Republicans hate him as much as millions of liberals. But nothing seems to work. I guess there are more bad Americans out there than I realized.

ISRAEL

Trump, in the last debate, was shocking in his refusal to declare a good guy and a bad guy in the Middle East. I mean Israel. He said he said, "Of course I am pro-Israel" but then he equivocated, saying he saw both sides of things in the Middle East, and would not play favorites.

He could negotiate a deal because he was an experienced businessman. Rubio laughed at him, saying this is not some real estate deal.

A few days later, black Muslim racist leader Louis Farrakhan praised Trump for distancing himself from Israel. Ebony and ivory, working together in perfect disharmony. The insanity never ends!

At least Farrakhan confirms that Trump had said a remarkably not supportive thing about Israel during the debate, even though he lied afterwards ("I'm definitely pro-Israel") after saying he would treat both sides equally.

Speaker of the House Paul Ryan, meanwhile, called a press conference to denounce Trump for not disowning the support of David Duke.

I voted for Rubio on Super Tuesday at the local middle school. On the wall of the room where I voted was a poster about bullying, how it will not be tolerated, and must be reported. Oh, so it's not tolerated in the schools, but it's okay if you're running for President. Now that is some unreal, tragic irony.

If Trump causes nuclear WWIII - which he easily could - then he is the AntiChrist!

SUPER TUESDAY

Donald Trump (I hate even typing his name) was supposed to sweep every state. But Ted Cruz won his home state of Texas big, plus Oklahoma, and Alaska. Rubio won the Minnesota Caucasus.

THE R DEBATE - 3.3.16 (RUDE)

As usual Donald Trump's rudeness dominated the Republican debate. But at least Ben Carson has dropped out.

Yesterday, 2012 Republican nominee for President, Mitt Romney, gave a rousing televised speech to a small group, outlining the case against Donald Trump for President. It was fantastic. And he said, 'What will Donald Trump say now in response to this speech. He will attack me, call me names, and will show again what kind of person he really is.'

Within an hour, Trump said that Romney was a "lightweight" a "choke artist" and a "failed candidate." The Republican nominee for President in 2012 won several states. It is scientifically impossible for Romney to be a lightweight.

If I was living in Germany in 1925 and my friends and members of my own family were defending rising star Hitler as being what's good for Germany, I might feel better with breaking up with some of them. Donald defends the Klan, and then denies it. The hoods are off. People cannot dare even say they don't like him without getting attacked. Young people in school are telling me the same thing. An army of bullies are gathering around the bully and doing his grass roots bullying for him.

Trump is a bully and a fascist who has NOTHING TO SAY, no specific plans, is a sexist, a xenophobe, and a megalomaniacal empty suit. He is not a man of faith, and is likely to cause the nuclear winter.

I mean it. I would lay down my life to stop this monster [as long as I died quickly.] 3.4.16.

CNN DEBATE - 3.6.16

I honestly felt like I saw something last night I had never seen before. In essence, Hillary exuded this message: 'This time I'm a lot stronger than I was in 2008. I've been Secretary of State, and I've also had enough of Bernie's attacks suggesting that maybe I don't hate Wall Street, which is his answer to everything. Well maybe I don't, and maybe you have to face things from a practical standpoint instead of offering extreme solutions to everything, solutions the Congress would never support you on, no matter how good it feels to say it.' - Not her exact words, but that's what is emerging. Sanders looked unglued to me at times and was cornered more than once - but he doesn't even seem to realize when he's been bested. Too much anger coming out of him and not enough joy. Trump and Sanders are both telling us that our country is in ruins.

I'm still a registered Republican, and I could support Cruz or Kasich. But Trump vs. Hillary? I would stand in a blizzard with a placard for Hillary. She looked like President Clinton to me last night and I never got that sense before. I think people can grow into the job and she's starting to feel it now, especially with Trump showing cracks in his armor.

SUPER TUESDAY II

March 9, 2016 was a "uge" upset win for Bernie Sanders in Michigan. Sanders mispronounces many words, and no one calls him on it because he is a Democrat. He beat Clinton by 50 to 49% in a squeaker. Michigan was winner take all, so that was a tough one for the two-fers.

Trump meanwhile rolls on, and I am so depressed about it. He won Michigan handily, and won Mississippi and Hawaii too. Has everyone lost their mind in this country? David Duke was a household name in America on the day a 25 year old was born, let alone a 69 year old man, which is Trump's age. Young people don't fully appreciate what a vicious lie Trump was telling that CNN reporter when he said over and over, "Who's David Duke, I've never heard of David Duke." In any case the earpiece thing in insane because he spells out that he heard the question correctly, so a miscommunication isn't even involved!

This makes everything so much worse. Now Sanders is going to keep hammering Clinton for being corrupt and dishonest, leaving her to stand wounded against Trump.

VIOLENCE AT TRUMP RALLIES

Day after day, the stories pile up. Fights are breaking out at Trump rallies. On March 12 a man tried to rush the podium, and the Secret Service leaped on the stage and surrounded Trump. It was the lead story on all the news. People I know have told me they would like to beat him up, and are not joking. Some want to do worse, and they look me in the eye and they are not kidding. No one has ever stirred up more hatred in this country than Donald Trump.

His rudeness is the reason I fear and hate him. His rudeness in international diplomacy would start WWIII. That's what I believe. Right now there's a less than one tenth of one percent chance of a nuclear war in the next 8 years. If he gets in it goes to five per cent. It is still likely we survive him, but the risk-math skyrockets.

Trump will stir up the lib-mobs. These lefties disrupt huge events in non-election years. With a REAL target, they are in a perfect storm for starting even more trouble.

Conservative is a lifestyle, not just a political leaning. A rude conservative is an oxymoron. That's why Trump is not a conservative.

TUESDAY MARCH 15, 2016

The ides of March for Rubio. The Senator lost Florida big to the thug, the liar the cheat, the racist, the misogynist. Trump also took Illinois and Missouri, which at first looked like it might go for Cruz.

Kasich won his home state of Ohio handily but that just means he won't quit the field, and the Republicans will remain divided and incapable of stopping the evil one.

Meanwhile, Hillary Clinton racked up wins in four states, putting an end to the great Bernie Sanders charge that his win in Michigan, the week before, got him back on a roll.

BRUSSELS AND ARIZONA

There was a major terrorist ISIS attack in Brussels on March 22. Trump won the Arizona primary on the same day. Sanders won Utah and Idaho caucuses, but it's too little too late for him, we think. Ted Cruz won the Republican Utah caucus.

MARCH 23, 2016 - NUKE ISIS

Trump on torture:

"I think we should at least almost level the playing field."

I haven't turned on a news channel for several days. I can't stand to watch it anymore. I can happen here. So I dared to peek in on CNN and the first thing I see is "Trump says he would use nuclear weapons against ISIS." And then the speech about leveling the playing field, and how no one has been as violent as ISIS since medieval times. Then I shut it off. I lasted two minutes. That's it. I only peek in on headlines via the internet the last ten days or so. Can't watch TV. Just concentrate on my history work, mostly the Revolutionary War and Vichy France.

BRUISED FEELINGS

Late in March, one of Trump's top aides was arrested and charged with battery for the way he grabbed a pushy reporter and forced her away from Trump. She showed her bruises to the press. Trump is standing by his top aide, and refuses to fire him. [I'm pretty sure this was Corey Lewandowski]

It was a typical case of a pushy reporter. The Trumpeter thug had been rough with so many people in recent days that he couldn't restrain his macho when he grabbed this female reporter.

Meanwhile the election is focused on some scandalous article about Cruz having an affair, and an unflattering picture of Ted's wife that Trump tweeted. The more Trump and Cruz have dramatic catty scenes about their wives, the more certain it will be that there will not be a Trump-Cruz ticket, which is my biggest fear (because I think it would win.) Keep at it boys.

APRIL 4 - WISCONSIN

Things are changing now. Trump is losing momentum. His flip flopping on so many issues is highlighting his shallow lack of knowledge on foreign policy; and his 8 months of insulting the media is finally catching up with him. The media held their shot while he insulted every reporter who dared to ask him a tough question and now they quietly fry him every day while he gets angrier and keeps losing momentum. Every poll in the nation has him still strong, but slowly losing ground with almost all demographic groups.

Tonight Trump lost to Ted Cruz in Wisconsin by about 45-35, with 18 for Kasich. Now the analysts are saying that a contested Republican Convention is more likely than not, maybe 60-40. Two weeks ago it looked like Trump could not be stopped, but when both the Democratic and Republican political machines are running attack ads on you all-day in 20 states and you give the ad producers tons of great new material to work with, you are in trouble; and he is.

But I still fear him as a third party candidate more than as the Republican nominee. That third party would be ugly. I'm sure of that. Plus he'd have the dictatorial control he so desires!

Meanwhile Bernie Sanders won Wisconsin over Hillary Clinton by about 54 to 46, but how he can win the nomination is hard to see. The two Dems keep attacking each other.

Ted Cruz is getting hot.

4.18.16 -TRUMP COURTIER ADVISES AGAINST CAL RALLY

Trump's courtiers had advised him to cancel two rallies scheduled for California this week. The main reason is the amount of anticipated protestors that will show up, disrupt the rally, and set off violence. Trump's rallies are like beer hall brawls in Munich in 1923. Almost all his rallies now turn into some violent incident. There must be a reason that this has never happened before in all of American history. Maybe the fault is not so much with his opponents as with the candidate himself. I'm no fan of disruption, in fact I'm against it, but there must be a reason why Jeffrey Lord and the other sycophants of Trump's Witenagemot are advising him to cancel. The benefits of a rally in California aren't worth the negatives from the disruptions. The violence and the hatred against Trump will be the lead story. The word is out that California, the state of protesters, will make the recent Trump disruptions in St. Louis and Madison Wisconsin seem like Trump-change.

These fascists have only one answer to their fear that their hate movement is losing power: More hate. One has issued a statement that he will give out the hotel and room number of any delegate who tries to block Trump's nomination at the GOP convention in Cleveland. In other words, a threat to get people beaten up physically if they don't to what Trump wants them to. ... Heil Don Hitler!

APRIL 20 - NY VALUES

As expected, Donald Trump won the primary vote big in New York State. I have stopped watching the news for a whole month. I don't want to see his face or hear his voice unless he wins it all. Then I suppose I'll give in. But he'll have to do it first. The other day in a speech, he referred to the awful tragedy back at "7/11." No Donald, it's 9/11. No one I know would ever make that mistake. He's old and he's just not that intelligent. He's not stupid, but he's no genius. 7/11.

As for the threats of violence at the RNC if baby doesn't get his bottle, Trumps tells the press that "I hope it does not happen" but he conspicuously will not call on his supporters to not be violent. In other words he enjoys and exploits the threat of it, while feigning to oppose it. I hate him. If he wins he will be the first truly bad person to enter the White House.

Sanders and Hillary had a vicious hate-debate a few nights ago. I can't stand him either. Her I'm beginning to like as the only sane candidate out there!

Hillary won 139 delegates in NY State, beating Sanders safely. That was a big blow to the big mouth of the left who thought NY might turn the whole thing around and put him ahead.

APRIL 26 - THE TWO EMERGE

I got a couple of anguished e-mails on the morning of April 27 from fellow Republican Trump-haters. My two Republican comedy comrades despise him. Trump had a huge 5-state sweep of victories in Delaware, Rhode Island, Connecticut, Pennsylvania and Maryland. Trump picked up 109 delegates and Cruz 5. Kasich won 3.

On the Dem side, Hillary Clinton won four out of five; and, in the one she lost, RI, she picked up 11 delegates to 13 for Marx.

It's looking inevitable for Clinton; and close to it for Trump.

Technically there is still talk that Trump may come up just short of the 1,217 delegates he needs to get the nomination at Cleveland, but I agree with him and his supporters that it wouldn't make much sense to give it to anyone else. What's the entire primary process all about if the man who wins 70% of all the total votes in the country is to be denied the nomination?

I hope he wins because he won; and I hope he wins because he will surely get clobbered in the general election. Polls now have him losing 50-30 with 20% undecided if he went up against Hillary one-on-one. The two of them have the highest negatives and the lowest positives in the history of polls for 2 front-runners. But it is what it is. I'm for Hillary and I hate Donald Trump. And I'm a registered Republican.

The other problem with rooting against Trump is that the alternative is Ted Cruz, and the left and his own party hates him. I don't share the hatred against Cruz. But now, the only alternative to the candidate that the Republicans do not want is another Republicans that the Republicans do not want.

Former Speaker of the House John Boehner said on April 27 that Ted Cruz is "Lucifer in the flesh," and the "meanest son of a bitch I ever worked with in my life."

Boehner said that Trump is a bad candidate who cannot get away with insulting everyone and expect to be president, but he said, reluctantly that yes, he would support him if he wins the nomination. But when asked if he would support Cruz if he were the nominee JB responded, "Over my dead body."

But Boehner then said something really stupid when he used the same cliché again. They asked him if Ted Cruz will become the nominee. Boehner responded, "Over my dead body," That doesn't even make any sense. That's like asking me, "Mike, are the Yankees going to win the pennant this year?" - "Over my dead body!" Now, if they asked me, "Mike, will you wear a Yankees cap on stage?" "Over my dead body," could make sense. The phrase involves something you have a decision on.

As for MSNBC, and similar lefty smug festivals, they are just as nasty, rude, and unfair as Fox is on the right.

I've had it with lefty know-it-alls, and righty know-it-alls. They are all so consistent it makes them untrustworthy. You know what their position is on every issue before the show starts.

Host Rachael Maddow is smug. She, and that attitude, says it all about why I'm a man without a political country. Where do I turn when I'm stuck between a Trump and a Maddow?

INDIANA

Trump won the Indiana primary on May 5. The next morning, Ted Cruz dropped out after a long fight. Ted Cruz started out on my bad side and ended up on my good side. Trump as of May 5 is the Republican nominee. Him I hate. I shut the TV off when he starts talking for more than four seconds. I can't stand the sight of him. He's the biggest liar of all time.

Bernie Sanders won in Indiana over Hillary, but he has no chance. Meanwhile Bernie shouts that he has a strong realistic chance. I'm just praying that it all works out, and, in the end, Trump is just another loser like George McGovern or Alton Parker.

I guess I'll be resigning from the Republican Party.

One thing never stops: The flood of words coming in from the rest of the world declaring that Trump is stupid and fascist, and you Americans are insane for even considering this guy.

GOOFUS

Trump's critics stress that he is childish, and it frightens them that such an immature volatile and unpredictable person could be in charge of the nukes. I feel that way. On May 6, 2016, he verbally attacked Massachusetts Senator Elizabeth Warren by calling her a "goofus" and a "goofball."

Elizabeth Warren is sometimes too strident for my taste, and she's a bit of a lefty too. But Elizabeth Warren is one of the most highly educated persons ever to step into the state of Massachusetts, let alone lead it, and she's formidable. She is not Rosie O'Donnell or Marco Rubio. She's tougher and smarter than them. I think Trump made a mistake kicking her like that. Trump needs to tone his act down and instead he hurls a below the belt and inaccurate spear at Elizabeth Warren. I'm not even sure how he means it, but I think it's because Warren kind of shakes her body when she talks. It's quirky, but not extreme, so it seems like he's stretching this quirkiness to reach out for another low class mockery of the handicapped, like before with the reporter; but it's just under the wire.

He is the worst thing in the world. I have never been more ashamed of my country in my life as I am to know that he is the Republican nominee for president.

And I know dozens of people personally who feel EXACTLY the same way.

I tell them I feel that way and they say oh yeah and then I say, "Look I'm serious. Not even the bullies in my childhood. I've never hated anyone or anything more. I'm totally serious." And over and over, people agree with me, just as seriously!

It is very upsetting to be in this spot in time and place right now. My personal life is fine. Still doing the comedy gigs, writing the books, doing the radio appearance, and I still love my wife. But with him looming on the horizon like a killer tornado, I do not feel happy.

MAY 10 PRIMARIES

The Republicans held primaries in Nebraska and West Virginia. Trump won easily.

Cruz and Kasich had dropped out. Cruz getting 18% of the vote in Nebraska after dropping out was an impressive showing. Trump is a shoe-in. Everyone supposedly hates Cruz, but he did all right with the voters. He earned my respect.

Bernie Sanders keeps scratching away, winning the West Virginia primary 51-35 percent over the Hillster. He has 1,433 delegates to Clinton's 1,716, but it's too late for Sanders to catch up.

"WON'T HAVE A GOOD RELATIONSHIP"

During the three weeks I liked Trump I was still disturbed by the fact that every signal coming out of Britain was angrily negative about him. That can't be a good thing for America if he wins.

In mid May-2016, Trump got into another (ho-hum) insult fight with a well-known person. That's his thing. That's what he does. He gets into rank fights with anyone who does not worship him.

British Prime Minister David Cameron had some negative things to say about the possibility of a Trump presidency, and Trump fired back at him:

"David Cameron has no right to say those things about me. He doesn't know me."

Oh yes he does. We all do. You're running for president and being exposed every day for everything you have ever said or done in your entire life, and your response to Cameron saying you are a hothead who would be dangerous when put in charge of nuclear weapons is "David Cameron has never hung out with me, he doesn't know me.'

The only time you aren't on film is when you're inside your own home. We know you. David Cameron knows you. What a poor defense.

The long and short of it is, after two days of rank-fights, including Trump making tough remarks about the Mayor-elect of London who is a Muslim, Trump admitted in a very public press statement that "I will probably not have a good relation with David Cameron."

Oh gee! No big deal. The Republican nominee casually admits that he will not have a good relationship with the leader of the USA's most important ally, and its best friend for more than 100 years. That's a deal-breaker right there. What's with his supporters? Even a righty interventionist conservative can't sanely hope that Trump gets in. Britain wants to vomit at the sight of his face, just like I do. Trump in office sets American foreign policy back on its heels. The day the puppet-bagger gets sworn in, Britain will turn elsewhere for allies. I hope he loses all 50 states and DC.

MAY 17 - KENTUCKY & OREGON

Trump won the Oregon Primary on May 17. The Dems had primaries in Oregon and Kentucky. Clinton won Kentucky 47 to 46%, and Bernie Sanders won in Oregon, no surprise there. The Oregon trail for Clinton was -12%. Bernie won 56 and she won 44.

CONTEMPT AND DISTRUST

There are so many thousands of people making comments I agree with about Trump, you can fill 500,000 words a day quoting them. If I tried to compile even some of it, I'd run out of fuel (time is fuel) for my other history projects.

The *New York Times* interviewed many Republican bank-rollers and concluded:

"Donald J. Trump wants to raise $1 billion. But hearing from more than 50% of the Republican donors, we found there is a measure of contempt and distrust towards him that is unheard of in modern Presidential politics."

Well yeah. Trump is contemptible and 100% untrustworthy. As for the rest of the Republican Party, yes, 33% like him. 33% hate his guts and 33% don't know what the hell to do.

Never say never, but I doubt he can win in November. There is small consolation in imagining one of the most humiliating defeats in the history of elections. All of his plans have been exposed by experts, liberal and conservative alike, as being vague at best and untenable at worst.

Now Bill Weld has weighed in. He was the governor of Massachusetts and is now running as VP on the 'Libertarian Republican' ticket. That's odd, I had never heard of a Libertarian Republican before now. I wonder how true Libertarian Party candidates feel about Weld and his Presidential nominee (an ex-governor, Gary something) stealing their titular thunder.

Weld said that Trump's immigration plan seems too much like Kristalnaught to him, but Bill held back when asked if Trump was a fascist. Weld said that he would not call Trump a fascist but he stands by the Crystal Night in Nazi Germany analogy nevertheless. (Crystal Night was when the Jews had all their windows smashed in for the premeditated crime of being Jews.)

MAY 24 - WASHINGTON STATE

Sanders is coming on strong. He beat Hillary in the 5.24.16 Washington Democratic Primary. Thanks, pal, for <u>electing Trump</u> by not giving up when unity is required. Thanks for your relentless attacks on Hillary, doing all the dirty work for the Trump people who can just sit back and mouth over and over and over, "thank you, thank you, thank you." Sanders is knocking her around senseless when she is the clear nominee. You selfish lefty pinhead fool! Soon it will be too late!

Out now!

GONZO - THE ARIZONA JUDGE - JUNE 5

I just did a show near Hartford with a comedian named Bill Campbell, who is not politically hateful on stage or off. We've known each other 38 years. He said to me, "I hate him more very single week."

I said, "You're doing better than me. For me it's every day."

The latest tempest is Trump's verbal attacks on the Arizona judge who is presiding over a suit against Trump University.

Trump has been suggesting that the judge cannot be fair because he is Hispanic and should be recused from the trial. Trump said that he is building a wall and therefore the judge will not be objective.

If that isn't racist, what is? Especially since the case has nothing to do with race in the first place! Trump's call for recusal is not only racist; it is an unequivocal rejection of the entire American legal system.

Trump should have backtracked on this point, but stubbornly defended his overt racism, and the gonzo story keeps snowballing.

The judge is from Indiana! His mother is Mexican and he was born in the USA! The case is about a Trump school accused of fraudulent practices. The wall is not relevant unless you presume the judge is a blind racist idiot. If Trump is right, if that judge should be recused, then no black judge can ever adjudicate a case involving a black person, and Judge O'Brien will overturn the jury verdict if Seam O'Mally is convicted of something. It's an insane and untenable position, intellectually, let alone morally.[2]

JUNE 7 - COLONEL SANDERS WONT QUIT

The polls for California in the last couple of weeks predicted a close race between Bernie and Hillary in California. Sanders talked of a big win in California and forcing the issue at Cleveland.

Well say good-bye to momentum, Bernie Sanders. Hillary clobbered Sanders in California on June 7: 60% to 40%, and by even more in New Jersey, a lefty state. It's all over, Bernie!

I watched on TV as Fox News correctly assumed that Sanders would come out defiant with a pledge to continue the fight. That's what they want. CNN analysts were unsure. Their analysts all speculated that Bernie might announce that he was suspending his campaign. That's what they want. Fox News knew best. Bernie came out and gave a rousing speech before cheering foot-lickers that he was not going to quit and will continue the fight, up to and through the Democratic Convention. Wild applause.

Thanks for being selfish, Mr. Ego. Democratic unity is the sure way to stop Godzilla Trump and you continue to divide the party and smash the Democratic front-runner with kicks and punches the R's can't match. Bernie's ego is as bad as Trump's right now, except that no one is calling him out for it. If he ends up running as a third party

---

[2] See back of the book for full text of the interview. It's beyond belief.

candidate, and I wouldn't put it past him, then Trump is the next President. Don't do it, Bernie!

Meanwhile Trump won a few more states with no one opposing him, and he gave one more lame speech, with no substance, to cheering fools; but for the first time he used a teleprompter. Trump has been ridiculing other candidates for using them, when he, on the other hand, gave his speeches off the top of his head. The ad libbing was leading to one verbal blunder after another, and he has finally listened to one of his 30 year old "senior" advisors with a lot of lipstick, and finally used the teleprompter. Someone has finally made him understand, at least for one night, that it might be wise to choose all your words carefully when you're the nominee.

Senator Lindsey Graham is pleading with fellow Republicans to withdraw their support for this man. One Republican after another is saying that Trump's statements are racism defined ... but they nevertheless are not withdrawing their support for the party's nominee.

KASICH ROCKS

I had mixed feelings about him throughout the race and I have feared that he would join a Trump ticket if invited. But John Kasich came through in early June with a very strong statement that no, he will not support the Republican nominee for president. I think that takes him off Trump's short list for VP.

OBAMA ENDORSES HILLARY

President Obama endorsed Hillary Clinton after she beat Sanders in NY and NJ. He then had a private meeting at the White House with Bernie Sanders, obviously an attempt to persuade Sanders to step aside and help Hillary Clinton beat Donald Trump. It didn't work. Bernie Sanders is so adored wherever he goes by lefty mobs, some of whom faint at the sight of him up close, that he can't let go. Left wing nuts are not notoriously humble. Neither is this one. He is intoxicated and has never experienced this kind of juice in his life. He's on a magic carpet ride and he is putting a monster in power.

Get out!

ORLANDO MASSACRE 6.12.16

On June 12 a Muslim-American went into a gay nightclub in Orlando, Florida, and killed 50 people. It was the worst mass shooting in US history. The sicko also wounded 53.

Meanwhile ISIS burned 20 teen-aged girls to death in a cage because they had refused to perform as sex slaves. So when adult gay men in America have consensual sex it's a crime against Allah. But when captive girls refuse to have hetero sex at knifepoint they are sinning.

This bad news probably helps Trump a bit. God how I hate him. He offended a lot of people when he Tweeted this about the Orlando massacre: *"I'm getting a lot of congrats in the I told you so department, but now we have to do something about it."* That was self-centered, weak, and not classy. Like everyone on earth doesn't know that these terrorist attacks are a regular thing now. He sets himself up as a swami because he warns they will keep happening. I predict that it will be windy in Chicago at least once with the next 200 days. You mark my words! Kudos to me if it happens.

He was getting <u>congrats</u>? Really?

TRUMP HITS THE POST

Donald Trump, unhappy with its criticism, has revoked the press credentials of the *Washington Post*. As of 6.13.16 the Posters can't attend his events or his press conferences. The baby doesn't get his way so he takes his bat and ball and walks off the field. He is a horrible human being.

The Huffington Post tweeted "Welcome to the club." Trump has banned the Huffies too. He tosses out major media outlets from his club like a big bouncer. By the time November 1 rolls around, Fox News will be the only media outlet allowed to cover him, and even half of those people hate him!

Trump is mad at the owner of Amazon because that villain also owns the Post. He is charging Mr. Bezos with purchasing the *Washington Post* only as a tax shelter.

So?

So what if it's true? Bezoz at Amazon isn't running for President, you are. Mr. 'I won't release my taxes because that would kill my chances to win' is accusing the owner of Amazon of doing something perfectly legal, in order to play with stats and beat the tax.

Michael Reagan, the son of Ronald Reagan is 100% correct when he says on any media outlets that will have him, "My father would never have supported this man, and would have refused to vote for him." Absolutely. Trump keeps comparing himself to Ronald Reagan. Ronald Wilson Reagan would have hated Trump. And it would have been a sorry day for Trump when he tried to intimidate Reagan.

This whole campaign has come down to, "He's horrible! - No! <u>She's</u> horrible!"

Wow. We're in for a rough ride.

TRUMP BACKTRACKS ON ORLANDO

I scoffed at Trump's quick suggestion after the Orlando night club massacre that if only people inside had been armed they would have shot back. Same old tripe from Trump. Anytime there's a shooting, he throws on his redneck hat and says that if only EVERYONE had a gun, this wouldn't have happened.

This idea makes sense emotionally, and there might be some truth to it; but my guess would be that having 600 young men in the nightclub packing heat and boozing it up every night would lead to far more deaths than lives saved at that one moment when a massacre was about to erupt.

Like everything else Trump suggests, it's not practical but it feels good to say it.

After a few days of negative backlash over Orlando, a tragedy which could have helped him, Trump has now said that what he really meant, of course, was that security guards at the club, and other club employees should have been armed. He wasn't talking about everyone on the dance floor.

Liar.

Besides, he used the exact words: "they'd be shooting back" and he has used them in a dozen other cases that he did not backtrack from. So we know what you meant the first time, squid. You are the worst thing of all time. The flag is flushed if you get in.

Now Speaker Paul Ryan is changing his mind yet again and saying he will support Trump. Actor Scott Baio is coming out for Trump. I give significantly less than 900 trillionth of a damn.

Trump fired his campaign manager. Corey Lewandowski, on June 20. Corey didn't get along with Manafort. Don has stopped bragging about his poll numbers, at long last. He can't even find one renegade slanted poll that has him ahead.

The other hot story is that Mrs. Clinton has $42 million in the campaign treasury and Mr. T. has $8 million. Why doesn't he just dip in to the $10 billion he's worth? Is that illegal? Can he just write a check to his campaign fund for $40 million and say, "There! Now we're ahead in campaign financing."

It's 44-38 Hillary in most polls, but that scares me plenty. There's a long road to go, and so much can happen. If the economy tanks, if there's scare in the Middle East, if she makes a poor VP choice and he a good one, and if he rattles her in the debates, he still could win. If this nation had a great soul, he'd be polling 8% nationally. To do all the hateful things he has done and still have 38% makes me ashamed to be an American.

SIT IN - JUNE 2016

I disapprove of this tactic, 100%.

US Senators and Congresspersons, about 100 of them, proponents of tougher new gun control legislation, staged a sit-in on the floor of Congress. They won't leave the building until new legislation, favorable to them, is at least voted on.

They're in the Capitol all night and refuse to leave. Catering trucks are coming by. They stage extralegal hearings and give extralegal speeches. It's all very 'mediagenic' and they know it: famous senators trying to force government action by physically taking over the floor of Congress like a Columbia hippie demonstrator in 1968.

Do you people think you can physically intimidate your own country into a certain action? You want laws to be respected. Start with yourselves! They are imitating Black Lives Matter tactics and they don't see what a hideous precedent this sets for the people, their constituents. If it's okay for them to resort to physical obstructionism to attain their political desires, it's okay for mobs on the street to follow the leaders.

BREXIT

Britain left the European Union in late June 2016, and pushed gun control (Orlando) off the front pages in America for several days. Prime Minister David Cameron is resigning over this.

No one in America wants to admit it, but I will. I haven't given four thoughts to the EU in the last 20 years. Britain leaves in a right wing nationalist move, and all of a sudden everyone is calling into talk radio ranting about how the sky is falling. Even SKYNEWS London said the sky is falling, and warned that the British pound will come tumbling after.

The American stock market took a fall, but mostly in the futures markets, which depend almost entirely on prices set in London. Wall Street, overall, has reacted with a downtrend, but how deep and lasting it is remains to be seen.

Trump flew to Scotland to look after one of his golf course investments and said that the Brexit was a good thing. It shows that people in England felt the same way about their country as he does about his. There's some frightening truth to this, but not too much, and, more important, reporters asked him a few weeks earlier about Brexit and the EU and he had no idea what the questioner was even talking about. Don is the biggest lair, phony zero of all time.

George Will, on June 25, resigned very publicly from the Republican Party citing Trump as the reason. Will is one of the most successful and famous conservative pundits of all time; up there with the big names like Bill Buckley and Pat Buchanan. Will's walk is fairly big news, even if it does get lost in all the mess of lame 'bulletins' about some washed-up Hollywood star endorsing or condemning Trump.

In any case, it's never about being for or against Hillary - these 'breaking news' flashes about endorsements or the withholding of them – it's only whether the person has come out for or against Trump.

I saw an incredible interview the other night on NBC News. The reporter called Trump out for saying that Hillary was sleeping throughout the entire afternoon of the Benghazi attacks, and missed all the reports. The reporter asked him if he'd like to retract the statement since there is zero evidence to support the charge.

He answered, "Well can you prove to me that she WASN'T asleep? She's a horrible person..." blah blah blah. The reporter was as incredulous as I was, just watching. The NBC guy just kept on Trump, trying to point out that he had made a 100% false accusation with no proof - and Trump childishly comes back with "Well she has been known to take long naps in the middle of the day when she should be working. So who's to say that she wasn't napping? I don't think these questions are very fair or very relevant."

The reporter gave up and moved on, shaking his head in disbelief.

I ask (as the reporter seemed to with his body language and facial expressions) how can anyone support this idiot? This pinhead? This simpleton? This bully? This racist? This super-phony? This I/me monster from Hell? Put on your thinking caps, America, this is the worst man in the history of Presidential politics. How is he still polling 38% after all the awful things he says does and proposes? He'd be polling 6% if the country had a brain.

He always has a plan that will change things "so fast it will make your head spin." I'd like to see Mike Tyson make his head spin. I hope he dies. Other than that I like him. Donald Trump is the embodiment of every negative human quality. Trump is from Olympus. He is the Greek God of Selfishness come down to earth in a human being.

ATATURK BOMBING

Ataturk Airport in Istanbul was the site of a late June 2016 ISIS terror attack. The brave troops of ISIS killed 40 tourists at the airport.

It's a terrible thing, but why does the media have to put an end to all other stories for about 72 hours whenever this sort of thing happens?

All of sudden, there's nothing on about the wars in Afghanistan, or the turmoil in Iraq. The presidential race is a distant secondary matter, only to be referred to as to how it relates to this far more important bombing story. One expert after another comes on and drones about what this means and what must be done and not one statement is of any use.

Only one professor ever nailed it, in my view. He said that terrorism is a sign of weakness, not of strength! If this is the best you can do, we should almost feel sorry for you as much as fear you. Terrorism is an admission that you have no political or military power: Otherwise you would use that, instead of terrorism.

Getting ourselves all worked up over every incident in the news is a dead end street. There's always something bad going on somewhere. The world population is now 7.4 billion. 15 years ago it was 6 billion. Bad things are going to happen somewhere every day.

Meanwhile, Trump gave an insane speech about all his business deals. "I make all kinds of great business deals. They're all great, even some of the horrible ones are great. I make horrible deals all the time, but they're all great."

That's a quote! Lawrence O'Donnell played the clip on MSNBC and I couldn't believe it. O'Donnell just looks at the camera and says, "These statements make no sense at all and appears to indicate some sort of insanity. Yet people still stand by him. I don't get it."

Neither do I, Larry. I hate being on the side of lefty MSNBC on anything, but this year it's all topsy-turvy.

FBI MAKES DECISION ON HILLARY'S E-MAILS

The Benghazi Report has cleared Hillary Clinton of any wrongdoing, and the FBI has decided that Hillary Clinton committed no crime when she carelessly sent thousands of government e-mails out through her private server.

The Republicans are furious and the Democrats are celebrating.

DALLAS ROBOT SAVES THE DAY - 7.7.16

The Black Lives Matter people were having a so-called peaceful protest in Dallas, chanting incendiary things while disowning the potential repercussions.

They were angry because a cop had killed a young black man the day before in a town I'd never heard of in Minnesota.

Suddenly a furious black man opened fire on police targets. He killed five of Dallas' finest. Other cops shot him dead before he could kill again.

Micah Johnson was a Gulf War veteran. He hated whitey and had been planning this for almost a year. Investigations revealed that he had a racial animus.

A peaceful protest is an oxymoron. Protest is stirring up trouble on purpose. There is no such a thing as a completely "non-violent" protest. It's a contradiction. Protest is not "peaceful," no way. Violent words are a call to violent action.

I protest the Black Lives Matter movement, and if you're mad at me now, it's because I just did something that was not peaceful. I protested.

I protest the idea that anyone thinks that protest is pacific. Protest is genetically violent.

Micah made history when he went down. The Dallas police used an armed robot to take him out. R2D2 had a bomb in his belly. The little robot tracked Johnson down and blew his metallica self up.

Hip hip, hoo-ray!

THE WALKWAY OF THE ENGLISH - JULY 14

A lone ISIL (Islamic State of Iraq and the Levant) terrorist ruined Bastille Day for France in 2016. The weirdo lunatic drove a 16 ton truck into a crowd of nice civilians enjoying the National Holiday in Nice. 86 people died and more than 400 were injured.

There is a famous Nice street called the Walkway of the English, which leads to United States Place. Just as the evening fireworks were ending, the evil fleabrain drove his truck through the crowd.

He was a Tunisian. He drove more than a mile while his truck was hitting people at 55 miles an hour. One brave motorcyclist managed to get on the sideboard and start punching him, but the loser knocked him off with the butt of his gun. The truck finally ran out of space and the police shot him dead.

TRUMP ENDS THE SUS-PENCE

I had greatly feared that he would name the venerable Newt Gingrich as his VP, and was relieved when he named Mike Pence instead.

Last night the late night TV comedians were all making jokes about how obscure this man is.

As someone who prays to God every night that racist bully Trump never becomes president I see this as a wonderful choice. Pence is the Governor of Indiana and has only a 40% approval rating in his own state. He's an old white guy who does not dye his hair. I fail to see what he brings to the table, although I know nothing about him and he might be stronger than I realize. I e-mailed a couple of smart political people, and they admitted that, they too, knew nothing at all about this guy.

Trump needed a woman, a black, a young energetic person, or a famous magnetic name for a Vice President. Why on earth would he pick an obscure white man from Indiana?

The answer is his ego. Trump would never want a political superstar for a VP.

Every few days one or two key polls show Hil & Don neck & neck, and I get depressed. But most of the polling patterns show Hillary ahead of Donald by about 42-38. That's the report from mid-July.

It is amazing to have a candidate renounced by the last two presidents of his own party, plus the last nominee. Two Bushes and a Romney are against him.

I've also been asking people in the know if it's legal to give a billion dollars to your own campaign. They say "I think it is, but I don't know if it is." I keep thinking it's a stupid question, but I'm getting nothing clear as an answer from some pretty smart people.

RNC - JULY DAYS - MELANIA VANILLI

Meet the next First Lady, Melania Trump! Night two of the Republican National Convention, in Cleveland, was supposed to give Don Trump a huge lift. When the American people meet Melania Trump, she will show that she is intelligent and articulate. She is nobody's bimbo! I actually feared a great Tuesday speech by Melania leading to a climactic positive finish by Trump on Thursday.

The lead story on the news on late Tuesday evening, however, was plagiarism. It seems that Melania Trump had delivered three or four minutes worth of oratory that was word-for-word stolen from Michelle Obama! MO's speech in 2008 at the DNC and Melania's in 2016 were identical in spurts.

At first I wanted to play devil's advocate, and defend Melania because I think the plagiarism charge is often really overblown. If two candidates three years apart say, "It's time we get this country moving forward again," the second person is not a plagiarist. It's too lame to even be called similar.

After reading the accounts (I refuse to watch the Republican National Convention at all this year - I know I would NEVER vote for Donald Trump, so why watch?) of Melania and Michelle's speeches it was plain as day embarrassing plagiarism.

This turned into a 36 hour news story and took away from Trump's message, which is 'I am in love with me, so vote for me.' It wasn't so much that this blunder actually damaged him or her. People felt sorry for her, she gave a good speech, and people understood that her speechwriters made the blunder. It was the fact that the new positive momentum did not happen that is the damage here. No one is changing their mind on their vote based on Melania ripping off the sitting First Lady, but momentum is key in these races, and he lost a chance to gain some.

Now a side-note on my sister Mary. She's not an extremely political person, but she is a hard leaning left liberal, although not a "lefty" which is a crusader that wants to pick a fight with everyone on everything on behalf of the left all the time.

Like many people, she was "afraid to bring it up with me." A lot of my liberal friends thought I might like Trump so they avoided the subject. Mary and I have talked about Trump and she now knows that I hate him. We agree that we cannot believe that anyone likes him. Mary Donovan is good friends with her boss. Her boss likes Trump and talks about him at work.

Mary drew the line. She told her boss, "Look, inside the office you can say what you want. You're the boss. But if you ever even so much as speak his name in my presence when we're out socializing it will be the end of our friendship."

I have told a couple of people the same thing. 'Look, I know you like him and I have no choice but to respect that. But if you want to still be my friend I'd advise you to not even mention his name around me.' That's how much I feel he is a threat to everything this country stands for.

What does that tell you that my liberal sister and I hate him so much that you not only should not praise him in our presence, you must not even speak his name? I know many people that feel exactly the same way. There has never been a candidate in the history of U.S. Presidential elections as despised as Donald Trump. Not even 1968's George Wallace who was dangerous and racist. But Wallace was not <u>personally</u> rude, uncivil, and egoistic; and was not ill-informed on the very subjects he claimed to feel strongest about. What they had in common of course, was, that they both had fathers who sympathized with the Ku Klux Klan.

MY HEROES - CRUZ AND KASICH

Ted Cruz and Donald Trump had a meeting in mid-July. It was private. In the end, TX Senator Cruz agreed to speak at the Republican National Convention. Everyone wondered, "Does that mean that Cruz is going to endorse Donald Trump?"

Cruz made it clear that it did not mean that. He didn't rule it out, but to me, he seemed to have made it pretty clear that he was more likely not to, but he would still address the Convention to show party loyalty, unlike Kasich who didn't even show up at the Convention, held in his home state.

Cruz addressed the Convention, all right. Cruz focused almost the entire speech on honoring the memory of the slain Dallas police officers. Cruz spoke of the orphaned 9 year old daughter of one of the slain. He talked about many things. But he did not endorse Donald Trump. Cruz mentioned Trump's name at the beginning, but only to congratulate him on winning the nomination. After that, it was all maudlin dead-cop talk and vague nothings about the great future of "our Great Republican Party." When Ted finally got around to saying anything of substance he shocked the crowd by telling Republicans everywhere to "vote your conscience" and only pick the candidates up and down the ticket that best represent what you stand for.

The crowd booed big time. Some fools cheered, not realizing what he was doing, and some cheered because they were part of the 'Dump Trump' movement. Cruz is a cool customer and smiled through the boos.

Teddy went back to vague rhetoric for a while. Then closed, amidst more booing, as he said nothing about Trump. By the end, everyone knew it was sabotage. Trump appeared at a side entrance near the end of the speech and the cameras went there. TV people talked about it, and speculated that Trump was trying to steal Cruz' thunder because Trump knew what was happening and was doing some damage control.

In any case, Cruz hurt him. Not that loyal Trump supporters needed a boost from Cruz, but Cruz has a lot of strong supporters who would reluctantly vote Trump if Cruz came out and supported him.

That's what you get, Don, for being so incredibly rude and unfair to Cruz during the primary debates. What did you think Cruz was going to do in Cleveland after you said last fall that Cruz is a "Liar and a nasty guy, a nasty guy," endorse you, wholeheartedly? Yeah, he is a nasty guy, and you crossed him.

So on Tuesday the story of the convention was Melania Trump the plagiarist; and on Wednesday the story of the convention of was Ted Cruz the obstructionist.

Now for the best part, the all-time infantile move. Trump announces the next day that he will not accept Ted Cruz' endorsement. "If he offers it, I will reject it. I will not accept any support from him." What a baby. "Ma, I want that candy!" "No!" "Well, Ma, if you offer me any candy I will not accept it because it comes from you! Do I make myself clear?" Yes, you do, Don. You are the biggest jerk in the history of American politics.

TIM

Hillary waited until the last day of the RNC to announce her choice for VP (it used to be that we learned of the choice at the convention itself, but now it's such a political football that even the timing is a weapon.) The new number two on Inauguration Day 2017 will be moderate Democrat Tim Kaine of Virginia (hopefully.)

Because Bernie Sanders[3] at least did not try to obstruct, after ripping her for 8 months, Mrs. Clinton had the option of looking to the center rather than feel she has to cater to the extreme left to please a protesting wing. Now the idea is to appeal to the independents, crossovers, and undecideds. Address the concern that some think she's weak.

The next Democrat VP might well be the next president. Most of us outside of Virginia did not know who he was when Kaine was named. We will know him down the line, I think, I hope.

AUGUST 4

Hillary is the nominee and as of today Trump is falling steadily in the polls. Ten days ago Trump had a two point lead and now she is nine points up in most polls, ten in a Fox News poll released today. Five points is a huge margin.

The DNC got under Trump's skin in a hundred ways, but especially when the parents of a dead Muslim-American soldier took to the podium. They condemned Trump as a man who would have this American soldier banned from the country. The father asked Trump angrily before millions of viewers, "What sacrifices have you made, Mr. Trump?"

Trump fired back with Tweets condemning the parents of the dead soldier. He really is mad at them. He said he has made many sacrifices by creating jobs, as if that makes any sense at all. The sight of his face makes me want to puke. I hate his guts. He is evil.

---

[3] Over the course of this book/blog I may have missed the moment when Sanders finally conceded and let Hillary be the candidate. I apologize for the missing link.

Once again, Republicans had to distance themselves from his statements. John McCain and Paul Ryan condemned his attacks on the father of the dead solider. Even Newt Gingrich is saying that Trump has to change his approach and that the last two weeks he has been "underperforming,"

Then you get his useless lackeys on all the TV shows explaining that Trump is not a politician and that's why the media hates him and why they pick on him, as if that's a great point. These Trump robots on the talk shows are pathetic. Their own candidate can't make any statements that make any sense, can't promote any decent logical and humane policies, only talks about I/me I/me I/me all the time, and then they have to go on TV and defend him.

I just watched 3 hours of politics on TV and all the Trump supporters are not even on the attack except on their own candidate! His own spokespersons are distancing themselves from his statements.

Every day it's a new self indulgent Trump ego-trip speech in front of white racist audiences in which all he talks about is how unfairly the media is treating him. It's a list of TV or newspaper people who wrote or said something about him that he thinks is unfair.

In the meantime all his smart backers are screaming at him to attack Obama and Hillary instead of being a baby and focusing on anyone who insults him personally. Maybe if they keep poking him and getting him mad, he will have a meltdown and everyone will see what a fraud he is, what a pathetic and weak man he really is.

Another example of his I/me sickness happened a couple of days ago when a veteran gave Trump a Purple Heart medal, the one the man had earned in blood, and said he was doing it to express his confidence in Trump. So what did Trump say about it? Did he thank the man for his service? Was he humbled? No, Trump joked around how, "I always wanted one of these. I didn't think it would be this easy." What a foolish, self-centered, and insensitive thing to say. People are digging in deeper into his draft deferments and his statements about it. He said that he got a very good number in the draft, and that's why he didn't serve. Zero truth to that. Apparently young Don had four college deferments, and one last one for bone spurs in his foot. Now it seems that there is no proof of any kind that he ever had a bone spur in his foot. It just went away by magic and there is no medical record of it. Mr. Tough guy. Mr. Jerk. You always wanted a Purple Heart? No one does. You always wanted to get an arm blown off?

Trump is now threatening to not endorse the Republican candidates up for election who are criticizing him. They are all aghast by his immaturity, his mental instability, his lack of manners, poise, or political insight, his hatred. Bombast and bluster got him through the primaries, but it's not working now when the idea is no longer that any publicity is good publicity. Five days of headlines over his feud with the father of a dead soldier is not the kind of publicity you need or want now, DT

I honestly thought he would cool it and put on a presidential act and make this thing scary close. He didn't, and for only one reason: he can't! Donald Trump cannot control his bad behavior. He got away with bullying everyone for so long that it's now an instinct he can't manage. He did everything in his power to make an enemy out of Fox News but, fortunately for him they still lick his feet because he's the only card they have. Commentators on both sides are in disbelief. The talk shows are in a stall with everyone just in awe watching him commit election suicide day after day.

Here is a man who is polling 2% among black voters, and still some people try and tell me that he is not a racist.

President Obama said yesterday in calm reasoned tones (something Trump is not familiar with) that "The Republican nominee is simply unfit to serve as commander in chief."

Agree. The first thing Trump would do is look for a war to start. Megalomania requires it. Donald Trump the worst American of all time.

A video was released today by two *New York Times* reporters who went to Trump rallies and filmed the people in the audience. It's scary. It's horrible. It's like a Klan or Nazi rally in spirit. Racial slurs, calls to kill Hillary Clinton, calls for a white America. It is an audience of Archie Bunkers and no one else. Can you watch that video and stand by that man?

OBAMA 54

I've been saying for months that Trump is making Obama look good. Sure enough Obama is now at 54% approval, the highest in his entire second term.

Everyone is so focused on the latest offensive racist bully remarks from Trump that no one is even talking about the "bad" presidency of Obama. I put it in quotes because I don't feel that way about him anymore. Compared to Hillary Clinton and the Satanic Trump, the devil himself, Obama looks all-right after all.

The latest good one about the bad one is the crying baby.

I've done at least 10 shows in my life when a crying baby interrupted the show. Two or three times the baby interrupted over and over. Each time I kept it light, and made jokes about it. I either minimized the damage or made it an asset by making jokes about how one of my jokes had obviously offended the infant.

Trump on 8.2.16 was giving another rally speech to an all-white audience of cheering rednecks with Nazi regalia hidden away at home when a crying baby interrupted him.

At first he said repeatedly (he always repeats himself) "I love babies, I have no problem with babies." Ten minutes and five interruptions later he made a jack-ass of himself yet again by snapping at the mother to "get that baby out of here!" The media had fun showing that clip, and I don't blame them. I'm happy to say that I am the last person on the plane to get mad at someone else's crying baby. I have a breaking point, yes, but for about three hours I am more annoyed with the people condemning the baby than I am with the crying baby. After three hours I'm fed up with the baby too, but I'm the last to break.

Obama keeps coming on TV and talking in calm reasoned tones about Trump's consistent unreason.

Trump is now saying over and over that if he loses, "the election is probably rigged."

What an evil man!

When asked to explain he goes into vague ramblings about voter fraud and people showing up to vote with no identification, and people baking the books, as if that would account for him losing 42 out of 50 states which is about how it's shaping up right now.

It's Don's sick answer to realizing now that he is probably going to lose. He rolls out his golfer's excuse towel in advance. If he wins, the election is fair. If he loses, the election is rigged.

First of all, if any party had been guilty of rigging elections in the last 20 years, it's the R's and that's your team, Don.

Second, as Obama says with bemused frustration at Trump's amazing stupidity: "The federal government has nothing to do with the election process. It is entirely operated by state, county, and town officials. The federal government can't rig an election, even if wanted to."

The amount of conservatives who are abandoning Trump and saying in public they will not vote for him is growing.

The jerk keeps slapping all his friends, enemies, and strangers around. More R power-people are coming out (with under 100 days to go) and saying they will not vote for Trump. Some say they will in fact vote for Hillary Clinton, others say they will not vote her as an alternative, and others say something else. But they are more and more saying that they will not vote for Trump.

Charlie Sheen is a famous actor who is also known for being political when he's not in a rehab. He's a conservative who likes to talk. Charlie went on a TV show and denounced Trump.

Sheen said that he had met Trump a few years ago and Trump made a dramatic gesture out of giving him rare and valuable cufflinks right off his shirt. Trump told him they were works of art made of precious metals and worth a great deal. This was a personal gesture he was making to Sheen because he liked him so much.

"Years later I'm moving and selling a lot of stuff. A jewelry appraiser was going through my wife's collection; and just as an aside I asked her to look at these cufflinks. She took a quick glance under a magnifier and recoiled with a sour astonished look. They were cheap garbage, not even jewelry. They were a consolation reward at a booth in an amusement park. We laughed it off, but now that he's running for president I would like to tell that story. I mean what does that tell you about the man?"

That he is a fraud, a cheat, a liar, and a man who cannot be trusted.

Cruz and Kasich saved the world! Imagine if either had begged in private to be his VP. He would have jumped on it.

For months my biggest fear is that he will re-invent himself shrewdly and act presidential until he wins and then the mask comes off again in order to start WWIII.

50 GOP SECURITY EXPERTS LETTER

This one made a little splash, the kind I like to see. 50 famous Republican national security experts drafted and signed a letter expressing opposition to Donald Trump for President. They said he was dangerous and mentally unfit to be commander in chief. They also said he was completely uninformed on all aspects of American foreign policy.

TRUMP CALLS FOR ASSASSINATION - 8.8.16

When I saw this clip I was shaking. He never gives his horrible act a rest. Trump said that if Hillary Clinton gets in she will nominate Supreme Court Justices and "there's nothing anyone can do about it, although the Second Amendment people might be able to do something about it." The crowd gasped and giggled, but it was awkward. A man in a red shirt and white hair in the crowd behind him opens his mouth in a big astonished oval and looks to his right at his companion with disbelief.

The Trump camp said that the remark was misinterpreted. What Trump was really saying, was that the 2nd Amendment people might be able to unite and use their political power to stop these appointments from reaching Senate confirmation.

First of all, Trump cannot think that deeply about anything and knows zero about the American political process. He is a complete embarrassing ignoramus. So the fake explanation came from someone who advises him who is smarter than he is.

Second of all, 99 out of 100 people, including me, who have seen the clip, feel that he is clearly joking about having either Hillary Clinton shot, or her appointees shot.

The media is running wild with this, and more Republicans are renouncing him and deserting the ship. The *New York Dailey News* called for him to call off the campaign. The former head of the NSA said that "If anyone else said anything like that in a public forum they would find themselves in the back of a police wagon." I could not agree more. Ordinary citizens who have called for Trump's assassination on social media have faced serious consequences.

Yes, he was making a joke. No one is denying that. It doesn't matter. It's completely unacceptable on so many levels. People do respond to thoughts like that with deeds. There's always some truth to the bent of a joke.

It's out of place to make those jokes when running for president at a public rally! There's a time and place to party like a devil, and a time and place to be staid. Standing in front of an audience of 800 people plus millions on TV while running for President of the United States of America is not the time to make assassination jokes.

As my friend said, "He is taking on water." Donald Chump is sinking big time. Now every poll has him down nationally by at least 10 points, and many solid R-red states have him at a dead heat. Romney took Kansas in 2012 by 20 points. A poll that came out just before the assassination gaffe had Trump 4 points up. That has to be 2 right now. Georgia and NC are a dead heat. So many people are coming out and saying, "I can't keep silent anymore." The list of Republican Congresspersons standing against him is up to about 16.

CBS ex-anchor Dan Rather has stayed neutral all year but he came out on 8/9 with a strong message that what Trump has done this time is beyond the pale, even for Trump.

And never forget, you lefties, it is we righties who are bringing him down! I spoke out about him on social media when he was the Vegas prohibitive favorite by 1-2 to win the election. Now he's more than a 3-1 underdog.

OBAMA FOUNDED ISIS

Every day he says something more absurd and offensive than the low thing he said the day before. On August 10, Trump spoke to his adoring audience of 99.99% white rednecks and announced that "President Obama is the founder of ISIS."

Right. The President of the United States founded the #1 enemy of the United States. Then he added that "Crooked Hillary is the co-founder of ISIS."

There is no let-up with this immature, despicable, immature, impulsive, erratic and idiotic man.

Most candidates see the adoring crowds on the campaign trail as a means to an end. To Trump, these crowds are the end in itself. This id-monster has never felt more at home in his entire life as he does in front of sycophant crowds that cheer his every word and laugh at his every vicious joke. He's never experienced this much personal adulation in his life. Until now he was the rich, flamboyant outspoken and sometimes controversial business man. But he never spoke to great adoring audiences like this before. Never. He can't fail because he is winning by being there. This is his dream come true. He is having so much fun! While the fate of the world hands in the balance.

And by the way, the charge against Obama, in a philosophical sense might make a tiny bit of sense. But Hillary? The Secretary of State implements policy; she doesn't make it. The charge makes no sense when it comes to her. As for Obama founded ISIS, how low can you go, bro?

Then the sycophant conservative media tries to help him by saying 'we know you don't mean that literally, but we see your point." "No!" says Trump, "I do mean it literally."

Donald Trump is the embodiment of everything I have ever hated in my entire life. He is all ego and has no love in him for anything but himself. I'm amazed by two things 1) That ANYONE can like him. 2) That he didn't name himself to be his Vice President.

TRUMP UPDATE - AUGUST 16

Now he's saying "Of course I was being sarcastic when I called Obama the founder of ISIS. The media doesn't know what sarcasm is, apparently."

Can you believe this toad? I can't. I saw you say it and stand by it. You were not joking.

One cannot keep track of all his offenses, and all the stupid things people say in his defense. The people on the internet who comment and argue in his defense are by an 8-1 ratio ruder than the people who oppose him. Sure, some Trump haters lose their sense of decency when they become enraged, but his supporters are rude and vicious and unfair when they are still calm. They are awful.

What is more astonishing is that his big-shot spokespeople are on TV day after day saying stupid things and making things worse. I'll give you one. A female Trumpeter on CNN yesterday defended the 'Obama founded ISIS' by blaming Obama "for bringing America into Afghanistan!" The CNN guy tried to give her some wiggle-room to back out of her error but she kept on and on about how Obama brought America into Afghanistan and how it "was Obama's war."

So this idiotic statement (W. Bush brought America into Afghanistan of course) dominates the news for two days. Trump loses a chance to recover from 40 errors of his own.

Then Trump starts saying that if Hillary Clinton wins Pennsylvania, it will be because she cheated.

Lunatic Ben Carson comes on CNN to defend an indefensible assertion. The CNN guy says how can you defend this statement?

Carson rambles on about how the main thing now is that we must all unite to make sure there is no voter fraud in Pennsylvania. The CNN man pushes the point as irrelevant since that's a universal that applies to all elections regardless of controversial unfair comments about the future. "What about what Trump said? Do you think that was wrong?" - Carson repeats his droning monologue about unity and the supervision of elections. The CNN man shakes his head and thanks him for coming on the air.

The regular anchors interview the Trump spokespeople and in the end they just shake their head, look at their co-anchor in disbelief, look at the camera in disbelief, and then with a resigned sigh say 'we'll be back after these messages."

The pattern is endless. Day after day, gaffe after gaffe, offense after offense.

National polls still have him only 3-5 point behind her. But in the really key keystone state of PA, she is up by 10 or more in all polls. Then Dump says the only way she can win is if she cheats.

Yesterday he gave a more articulate speech about foreign policy, but it was so not him, so contrived, so written by his righty general Mike Young, that it really was sickening. You're trying to reinvent too late. Teleprompter Don is even more disgusting than ad lib Don.

AUGUST 17, 2016

The teleprompter act continues. Trump is sounding tenth grade poised in making his latest speeches. It's so incredibly forced. Every intelligent sentence is obviously written word for word by one of his latest advisors. They have convinced him to stop attacking the media and stay on message about national security and the weaknesses of Hillary Clinton. Or to try to ... he can't help himself. The real lunatic always bursts through at some point.

Yesterday he threatened the voters of Pennsylvania that "If they do not vote for me in November, I will never ever forgive them."

Incredible. This one actually had me laughing out loud so badly I worried that I would disturb by condo neighbors. "You people who just let me know that you disapprove of me in a fair election, I am never going to forgive you." We have never seen more concrete indisputable proof that Trump is sick with ego.

APOLOGY TIME

Trump knows he's toast so his new campaign manager Steve Bannon, clearly a very bad human being, just like Trump, has advised Don to back off and apologize weakly as a gesture of strength and a desperate move to save the sinking boat.

So Trump made a speech on August 18 in which he stiffly and formally said he may have somewhere along the way "chosen the wrong words" to express himself and "believe it or not I actually do regret this" especially when it might "have hurt some people." Then he gave a short fake smile that really expressed anger.

Gee, Don, could you be specific?

Of course not. That would count for something.

Anyone can make a vague apology across the board. An apology counts for nothing unless it's specific. Being nonspecific mans you get all the glory for humbly apologizing while paying none of the tough price of a genuine one.

Besides that, Trump means every mean word the mean machine ever says. It's not a matter of a poor choice of words every time. You go out of your way to be mean to countless people who deserve respect, and when you see that Hillary is up by 14 pts in traditional Democratic Virginia you decide now to make an apology.

Trump looked like he was in pain when he did this sort-of apology out of desperation, off a tele-prompter, obviously not one word written by him. When he finished he probably went backstage and smashed something.

ONE BACKTRACK AFTER ANOTHER

With one week left in August, the polls haven't changed much. They either show it real close; or Hillary holding a lead of 6 -8 pts. No polls have Trump with a big lead.

With new devil management, Trump is backtracking on all of his major positions. Now he thinks he can find some path to allowing illegal immigrants to stay in the country without first being deported! That's been his number one tough-guy issue from day one and all of a sudden he's sounding like Obama. It's the same on many issues. The new managers have finally explained to him that he is certain to lose unless he starts lying and pretending to be a nicer guy. "Then when you get in, you can go back to being a jerk again." If he had played that card much earlier it might have worked. But now ... But it's not close to over and I'm scared for the flag if that monster wins. He's the American Hitler, no doubt about it.

Saw a hard hitting attack ad on Trump on August 24. It talks of how we need a calm hand on the nuclear trigger and shows Trump at his worst in three clips.

1. He tells his security people to beat up the guy they are escorting out of a Trump rally - "Rough him up a bit, that would be great, really."

2. They show him at a formal podium shouting like mad-man. "So you can tell them all to Go (beep) Themselves!"

76

3. They play a radio clip of him saying "I would just bomb the (beep) out of them, that's what I'd do."

That about sums up how insane it would be to put this human stain in charge of the nukes. I approve the ad, but this might win too much approval from voters it's supposed to dissuade. I would always include him doing the handicapped reporter pantomime, and the three times denying he knew who David Duke was.[4]

SEPTEMBER 16, 2016

It's been a relatively quiet three weeks since my last I hate Trump confession. The polls have really tightened now, thanks to Hillary's health issues. They are getting serious. She's had some coughing fits while trying to make a speech. I mean real bad. Worse than anything I've ever seen happen to an ill comedian ever.

Then she made a speech at the 9/11 memorial on the anniversary of that tragedy, and she collapsed. She had to go to a hospital.

Sure enough, just a few days later, the polls in the swing states have Trump ahead by a couple of points after trailing for months. Of all the horrible unforeseen setbacks.

Now she <u>has</u> to have a good debate against the corrupt racist thug.

This is getting really scary. He's the worst person that ever lived and he might be president of the greatest country on earth. The USA will no longer be that, the day he gets elected.

A 14-page article came out in *Newsweek* about the Trump empire. The empire is mysterious; it's world- wide; and he's got his hooks into creepy connections with countries all over. The article reached some awful conclusions about his wealth, where it is, what is unknown, and how his money empire would create a total conflict of interest between his personal, and America's national interests.

---

[4] The new ad I mentioned was saturation played right to Election Day, to the exclusion of almost all other ads. My suggestions about the Duke clip and the handicapped reporter never happened!

EVE OF DESTRUCTION

Ted Cruz came out in mid-September and endorsed Donald Trump. Now I hate Ted Cruz. I liked him for so long. Any politician who endorses Trump is a no good bum. Oh, and now it turns out that Chris Christie did indeed know about all the New Jersey bridge closings.

On the eve of the first debate, the polls have Hillary and Mr. Bad in a tie. I can't believe this is happening. Trump is the most horrible man in the world!

THE FIRST DEBATE - SEPTEMBER 26, 2016

The main thing was that Hillary showed up and looked and sounded healthy. Her pneumonia scare took her six point lead and wiped it out. She was sure to score some points just by looking okay, and she looked and sounded fine.

Trump kept making some sort of sniffle noises, and no one in the post game show seemed to notice.

He was a rude, obnoxious bully all night, and she was poised and articulate. He was frantic, like he was guzzling gallons of super-caffeinated coffee all day. He kept interrupting her, bullying her over some lame basic point he drilled home as though it were some irrefutable gem. The big lame mantra was "NAFTA was a disaster!"

Hey pal, that's not a fact, it's an opinion and some people still like it. The North American Free Trade agreement was passed 20 years ago. That's like arguing about the Cuban Missile Crisis in 1982.

The main thing is the yelling at her and the interrupting. What a hideous human being.

He stumbled on his words, and his tirades were rambling and incoherent. He stuck to simplistic points and lame generalities while she made an effort to at least have a little something to actually say. He said nothing but the sky is falling and everything is "a disaster, believe me."

She destroyed him from start to finish, and most of the polls today say that she won, although not to the degree I think she won, which is about 10-1. She's a decent, intelligent, courteous speaker. He is an indecent, stupid, and discourteous speaker. I could feel my body shaking with anger at him the whole time. I had to shut it off after 30 minutes and go take a walk. I caught up with it later on the TV recorder.

So many offensive moments for him. She exposed him over and over for the bully hypocrite racist ignoramus he is.

Moderator Lester Holt lost holt of the debate. Trump kept scolding Holt for interrupting him. "You asked me a question!" Holt kept trying to call Trump out for his lies and Trump would *scold the moderator.* Wow.

My favorite was when Holt asked Trump how he could keep his campaign promise to bring the companies that left America, back home.

"Well Lester the first thing you have to do is not allow them to leave in the first place and blah blah blah."

"Well I know sir, but how do you get them back, the ones that left?"

"Well first of all you don't allow them to leave in the first place."

This went on two more times before Holt gave up on the dolt. Trump's idea of logic is insanity!

When Hillary called Trump out on his racist birther movement, I had tears in my eyes. She talked of how she saw up close how much the whole thing hurt Obama's feelings, and now Trump claims he did the country a great service by forcing him to produce his birth certificate. But Don, no one else but you and a bunch of racist right wingers ever thought this was an issue to begin with. You create a racist crisis then claim you did the world a service because it settled down when you were proven wrong.

Hillary pointed out that Fred Trump had paid a huge fine for racial discrimination in his housing units in the 1970's. He yelled back that he never admitted to any guilt!

Hey idiot, that's part of the deal when you pay off. If you went to trial you would be called guilty or not guilty: but paying the fine makes guilt irrelevant, but also implicit.

What a dirty rotten cutthroat liar!

I was a FOX News watcher in 2012, now I won't watch those Trump-lickers ever. Not at all. Not even during the commercials of the football game.

TRUMP SNIFFIES

I wrote after the debate that he had some sort of sniffles and the post-game analysts didn't seem to notice.

Well, plenty of other people did. There are now compilations of his 30 loud sniffs during the debate. So what did Trump say about it? He said it didn't happen and that there was some defect in the microphone that made the sound.

Are you kidding me? What a blatant lie! Why lie about that? What are the odds that in the biggest TV event in all of American history, an event watched by more people than any Super-Bowl, the people running the show are going to put up a microphone that would annoy me at a VFW gig in Tewskbury?

Howard Dean, the front-runner for President for a few weeks in 2008, Tweeted that Trump might have been using cocaine.

There was quite the backlash against Dean for this comment even from his own left side, but I was thinking the same thing. I was thinking that, sniffles aside, this guy seems like he's all coked up. I've been around countless numbers of coked up people. I never touched the stuff, but I know a coked up person when I see one and Trump acts like one quite often, and in every way.

Social media is all over the "Trumpsniffie" issue, even if the mainstream media is in denial. Why does he deny it even happened? Just like when he said over and over "I have never heard of David Duke" and then two days later said that there was something wrong with his earpiece and he didn't really hear the question.

Trump is a threat to everything that is decent and kind in America. He does not have a compassionate bone in his body and he does not know how to laugh. He has never ever laughed and I keep looking for it. He has a smile, but no laugh.

Someone should ask him for a hair sample so he can pass a drug test, just like post office workers. Trump supposedly doesn't drink. But can a famous playboy womanizer like him really go through life without a vice? If Trump isn't doing cocaine, then he sure does a great impression of a person on cocaine.

WORST WEEK

The debate and the week following it were bad for Trump. I really cannot keep track anymore of all the horrible things he says and does.

For starters he told everyone that all the polls clearly indicated that he won the debate, a total lie. Then he got into a 'Twitter fight' over Miss Universe.

Near the end of the debate, Hillary Clinton brought up his verbal abuse of a Miss Universe contestant. She had put on 30 pounds. He'd called her a "disgusting pig" and reduced her to tears. He'd made her so depressed that she went on an eating binge and put on 20 more pounds and lost her modeling contract ... or something like that.

So Trump goes after Miss Machado's personal character on social media, rather than address the issue of his being a verbally abusive sexist. He Tweets off and on all night that Machado "is no angel" and Twit followers should "check out her past, just watch the film."

What film? So the press looked into her past and found that Machado had once been in a soft-core adult film (no explicit scenes) and guess who else is in it: Donald Trump! He kept his clothes on, thank Allah, but, turns out, he had a role in a porno and he's Tweeting all night about her lurid past. The more he Tweeted the more everyone except his ardent supporters laughed.

On October 1, Trump gave an 80-minute late night speech in Montour, Pennsylvania (I watched it) in which he added more rude demerits to his record. He made a mocking pantomime of Hillary Clinton being unable to make it to her car. The former First Lady had visited the 9/11 Memorial and had a near collapse a few weeks earlier. It was pneumonia and she was well over it now. The debate had proved it.

He made fun of her with an act-out of her unable to stand and slouching over in agony. That's something a Nazi would do.

Then he went on to use the term "blood-suckers" to describe big business cheating the working people.

Wow. That word really made the hairs stand up on the back of my neck. I have almost never heard that term invoked in modern political discourse in America. Maybe never. I think Farrakhan uses it to describe the Jews. One place I see that word all the time is in reading the writings of the Nazi Party, which as an historian, I have done. The other place I see that word all the time is in the famous Stalin book, *The History of the Communist Party of the Soviet Union*. Stalin was the head writer on a loyal staff, and the word 'blood-suckers' is used often against political enemies. So we have Hitler, Stalin, Farrakhan and Trump, the only four people that like the word, "blood-suckers."

No sooner does he bash the "blood-suckers", than the *New York Times* gets their hands on his state tax returns from 1993. Trump, the man who brags and brags and brags about how rich he is, and how successful he is, reported a net loss of $916 million dollars in 1993. That way he doesn't have to pay any federal taxes for the next 20 years.

So he's bagged as the biggest hypocrite of all time. The media digs up about 20 clips of him being viciously critical of other people for not paying their fair share in federal taxes.

How does he worm his way out of this one? Next thing you know, Trump admits it, admits that it was barely legal, but "It proves I'm a genius, frankly, if you want to know the truth. I am. Believe me."

His foot-suckers Jeffrey Lord and Rudy Guiliani all back him up, "It proves that he a genius." Then they call out the critic saying, "Don't try to tell me that you don't take every tax deduction possible!" So what - Who cares? I'm not running for president and they are two totally different situations. All of a sudden Mr. Law and Order Guiliani is invoking "we all cheat; who is kidding who?"

Disgusting!

Trump won't release his tax returns and the last thing in the world he wanted anyone to know was that he lost a billion dollars in 1993 and that he used these losses to brilliantly avoid paying federal tax.

It would be one thing to be open and explain that you are so smart that this is how you make the most of the tax laws, now vote for me because I'm so smart. What smells bad here is that he never would have wanted anyone to know this, has criticized others for not paying taxes, is championing his selfless patriotism every day, and refuses to release any tax records. Then we find this out.

VP DEBATE

I guess I'm just biased now. A few night ago, *Saturday Night Live* did a spoof of the first Presidential Debate. Alec Baldwin skewered Trump, and someone I don't know made fun playing Hillary. For once the unfair bias worked in my favor. The pot-shots at Hillary were very moderate in viciousness, and they went after Trump ten times worse.

Good for my friends at SNL that I've resented for the last 25 years. I'm glad they are their good ol' reliable lefty selves this year. It was hilarious. Basically, Alec just made fun of Trump's infantile nasty ways.

On September 4, the first Vice Presidential debate pitted Republican Mike Pence against Democrat Tim Kaine of Virginia. Most polls said Pence won the debate. He looked more the smooth articulate leader than Kaine, I'll grant you that, but Pence not one time could defend one single position of his boss Trump that Kaine called him out on. Pence chickened out on every challenge regarding Trump, then, near the end, denied that he had done so and challenged Kaine to name the charges, one at a time.

Doyeee! He already did.

Pence was a liar, just like Trump. He said that ISIS had overrun Iraq.

Wrong, Mikie. Most of Iraq is now secure and ISIS is falling back towards Mosul. This is from a CNN fact-check, not from me.

I posted on Facebook that "Hillary is 100 times better than Trump. He is the worst person in all of American history." I ruffled a few feathers. I'm tired of being bullied by Trump lovers and Hillary bashers. He is. He is worse than Joe McCarthy, Aaron Burr or Benedict Arnold; Worse than Charles Manson. A Trump presidency would increase the risk of a full-scale nuclear war times 20.

GRAB HER BY THE

September 7-8 was the great implosion. An audio tape of Trump bragging backstage about his sexual assaults on women has taken his campaign down big time. I am writing on the afternoon of the second debate, September 9.

This story broke and I heard the tape. I hear what is happening, sociologically: he is trying to impress a young man with gutter talk about how he gets to start kissing women without asking. He brags about hitting on married women. He brags about how he likes to "grab them by the pussy." Not during sex, mind you, but as part of his pick-up technique. "I grab them by the pussy. I'm so famous, they let me." The enabler, TV host, Billy Bush is giggling and encouraging Trump to keep talking the locker room talk.

More Republican United Senators have now disowned him. It went from about two to about 15 overnight. That is serious business. For a while a couple of lesser known senators had disowned him and the rest had swallowed their anger and endorsed him while denouncing many of his statements. Now they are denouncing him. Republicans all over the country are saying, like me, that they will vote Democratic in this election. John McCain has disowned him.

Robert DiNiro has made a video verbally attacking Trump and saying he would "like to punch him right in the face"

So Trump came on yesterday with an apology that ended with him attacking Bill Clinton and saying that what Clinton did was far worse and we'll see you at the debate Sunday night.

Trump was supposed to appear with Speaker Paul Ryan yesterday in a key display of reconciliation and harmony. Ryan disinvited Trump. The Republican National Committee is not defending him. It is de-funding him, making him pay for his own mailings. Senator Mark Kirk, a prominent Republican leader, called for the Republican rules committee to explore a way to force Trump off the ticket!

Vice Presidential nominee Mike Pence is angry and is nowhere to be seen. All of his speaking gigs have been cancelled for the time being and there are rumors he is going resign from the ticket! People on both sides of the aisle are now shouting for Donald Trump to resign from the top of the ticket. I am shocked on Sunday to see the political talk shows chatting it up about how the only clear choice for him now is to resign! Trump is issuing statements that "I will never resign!"

When that is the state of your campaign, you are in a lot of trouble. "I will never resign!" 29 days left in the campaign and Don's own party is screaming at him to step down from the ticket! It's really incredible.

Then I'm reading a statement from a female Trump, and I do get them mixed up, and I'm presuming it's his daughter saying "I am deeply offended by his insulting remarks. I hope people will accept his apology." Then I read closely and it's his wife! The wife of the nominee for president is issuing a statement that "I was deeply offended by him!" What episode of *The Twilight Zone* am I living in? Melania, after being offended by her husband's words adds, "But that is not the man I know." - What? - T-Zone music, please.

Donald Trump did the same thing. "I'm sorry for the words I used. But that does not represent the real me." Of course it does. They're your words. What are you, some sort of an imbecile? Whose words are we supposed to judge you by, the Mayor of Yellowknife?

THUG DEBATE #2

The second debate was as disgraceful as the first. Trump was physically looming behind Hillary, walking around like he wanted to physically attack her.

ISIS THREAT

Trump said today that "If Hillary Clinton is elected ISIS will take over this country!"

He keeps threatening to put her in jail.

The latest Trump TV ad is the lowest. It shows clips of Hillary coughing and being helped into a limo as she stumbled from being ill the day she visited the 9/11 memorial. That is the lowest thing I have ever seen! He now is harping on how if he loses, the election is rigged. He is fighting with about 80 members of the GOP, and defections are increasing every day. Of the 50 major newspapers in the United States, not one is endorsing him. Not one.

People are scared that he might incite his people to great violence if they are on the verge of a 50 state loss. The latest polls have him down by an amazing 14 points.

Two women have come forward saying that Trump touched them inappropriately.

WHY DON'T YOU SAY IT TO MY FACEBOOK

I'm getting now from Trumpeters on Facebook is - "Bill Clinton's a rapist!" "Hillary's an enabler!"

Where was this panic over Hillary the enabler when she was a Senator and Secretary of State? Now it's a crisis that this "enabler" might get in. If she is so unfit for president, for this reason, then why no outrage when she was at the top of the State Department? I'm not voting for her husband. He's not running for president. She is. I did not vote for Bill Clinton, and never even considered it. You want to call me out for defending Bill Clinton? I never did. My history book on him is not supportive, so I've nothing to defend. That was then, this is now.

I feel sorry for most Trump supporters. If you're hard right, it's tough to not back him as the lesser of two evils. I spent three weeks on the bandwagon before I realized he was not just cruel and immature, but breathtakingly uninformed. He clearly is not a mature individual. Tell me something good about your candidate once in a while, instead of always attacking Hillary. The only thing to grab on to is that he is a highly successful businessman, and now that even looks shaky. If I'm alive in 2020, maybe I'll be backing a Republican I like and some of my lefty friends will be mad at me. That will be then, this is now. Right now I am smack dead in the center of lefty-righty and I don't have any trouble backing a moderate Democrat, who is far superior to her opponent in every way.

GO AHEAD - MAKE OUR DAY - SUE US

Donald Trump is threatening to sue the *New York Times* for ruining his reputation. *Times* printed stories from two women claiming that Trump touched them inappropriately. The incidents happened a while ago. It's Bill Cosby all over again. The women knew that the person who violated them was too rich and powerful to defeat in court, and then when the giant is tottering from similar charges from others, they break their silence and come forward.

Trump the thug has been threatening to sue anyone who crosses him since he was about 19. Now he has met his match in the *New York*

Times, which issued a scathing statement saying, "Mr. Trump, you have no reputation. How can we slander it? You have already boasted about this behavior. We did not say these stories are true, we are reporting the story as is. We look forward to seeing you in court." That's close to their exact words.

Trump has threatened to sue many people since this campaign began. He hasn't sued anybody.

Trump is unraveling and threatening a revolution if he does not win. The election is rigged if he loses, but it's honest if he wins. Translation: the sooner he leaves this earth the better.

Michelle Obama and her brilliant husband, my president, gave great speeches yesterday (9.13) and then Trump gave a real thug Nazi one, filled with clear hints of anti-Semitism. The media was aghast at his Hitlerian complaints about the international money conspiracy and blood-suckers trying to throw this election for Hillary.

The Nazis are taking over. The entire country is upset.

A Chinese-American cashier at the supermarket next to my house has been away for a few months. I saw him yesterday and asked him where he's been and how he's doing. His name is Hai and I never saw him like this. He was so down, so defeated, so despondent. I couldn't believe the look all over him. I probed a little and he told me he could not believe that people still are supporting Donald Trump. After all these horrible things, how can he still have any support at all? I never saw him like that.

He's deeply hurt. This basically cheerful cashier is totally consumed with a deep dark depression over this, and so am I. Don is the biggest jerk ever. One out of every 7 people on earth hates his guts. There's something to be proud of.

President Obama is really hitting stride. His oratory, his confidence, his sincerity, his moral compass, has never obviously been better. What a speech he gave yesterday to a nice respectful audience.

"You Republicans claim to be the party of family values. And this is the guy you nominated? - You claim to be tough on national defense. You'll stand up to the Russians better than the Democrats. And this is the guy you nominated?"

I watched this speech at 4 am on my tablet with tears rolling down my face.

The cover of *Time* magazine just came out and the cover is a cartoon of Trump's face melting, and the cover said, "Total Meltdown."

A new video came out showing him talking to a ten year old girl. He asks her is she's going to ride up the escalator. She says yes and departs. Trump turns to the camera and say, "I'm going to be dating her in ten years. Can you believe it?"

Today a new tape has him saying, regarding the rehab-riddled life of actress Lindsey Lohan: "Deeply troubled women are always the best in bed."

His past is catching up to him at crunch time. The old story of no matter what he does, his base will still support him has taken a hit on the white female side. White female Republicans usually support their candidate by more than 90%. New polls are indicating that 70% of white female Republicans are now supporting him. 70% might look strong on paper, but that is a big hit because the drop off of 20% comes from within the core of your power base. Old white stupid racist angry redneck men will still support him, but now a significant percentage of white redneck women are even dropping out.

He is the embodiment of every evil quality that a person can have. And people are becoming aware now, that there will be violence if and when he loses.

Trump is so rehearsed in his speeches now. They are more vicious than ever, but they are clearly better written than before. He used the word existentialist yesterday and I'm confident he didn't even know what it meant 6 months ago. He speaks more slowly and deliberately now. He might even be rehearsing his speeches. The Breitbart bullies are trying to put a suit on this gorilla. His message is more vicious than ever, but his delivery is more formal, more ostensibly articulate. Gone are most of the vicious cracks off the top of his head.

So many people are giving so many great speeches against him that I am in awe of them and can't begin to list them all. Chris Matthews and Keith Olberman gave a couple of great ones yesterday. Both were very emotional in denouncing his threat to put Hillary in jail. What kind of stain is this man, and how did he get this far?

When he was over the top rude to all his Republican opponents in the early debates, I was shocked that a week later he was still even standing. I'm with president Obama condemning the Republican apostates for waiting this long to drop off.

The only reason I haven't changed my registration from Republican to Independent is because the form isn't in front of me to do it. Obama is right. You waited this long to be offended? You don't deserve medals for dropping out now. It took this tape to offend you, after all he's said and done the last year and a half?

Hitler died in 1945. Trump was born in 1946. The two men never walked the earth at the same time and I believe in reincarnation.

TRUMP DEMANDS HILLARY TAKE A DRUG TEST

Trump is making speeches now demanding that Hillary take a drug test before the next debate because she clearly is on amphetamines (performance enhancing drugs.) Mrs. C is jacked. He says that she had a lot of energy during the first half of the debate, but at the end (he mocks her in pantomime) she was lifeless, "couldn't make it to her car."

Evil and inaccurate on many levels. If she can't afford amphetamines that last more than 80 minutes, she needs to find a new dealer or pharmacist - Besides, I saw the debate; not true at all, and he himself said at the end of the debate that he respects her because she keeps on fighting no matter what.

OCTOBER 17, 2016

I can't keep track of all the vicious crazy things he says and does. The reporters just stand back in awe as he threatens them. Now he's having a breakdown in rage over the *Saturday Night Live* spoof of him. Trump tweets that Baldwin's impression of him stinks and that it's time to retire this unfunny show.

You were just on it!

I'm a professional impressionist and have worked Vegas. It's a solid good impression. It's not Rich Little, but it's passable professional quality and it's also funny. Baldwin captures the inner soul of Trump. Baldwin is "feeling it." Trump is wrong. It's a good impression.

Now granted, the show isn't funny most of the time, but one sketch a show rocks, and I think the show still has a future, Don. A better one than you do.

Former New York Mayor Rudy Guiliani was once a hero to me and now I have lost all respect for him. He and his nasty apologism speeches make me sick.

Now Trump is going on and on about the impending voter fraud. The election is rigged. There is going to be massive voter fraud on Election Day.

Everyone in the know is trying to tell him, and the public, that the chance of a vote in the USA being fraudulently tabulated is a million to one. You have a better chance of being struck by lightning than having your vote miscounted. Independent study groups are coming up with numbers like 45 or 72 in the total number of fraudulent votes proven cast in a given Election Day in the recent past. That's out of 80 million votes.

He keeps shouting at rallies that the election is rigged. These statements are flat out sedition and fascism. The country and the world are horrified and his numbers stand tall at around 40%. This thing isn't over. I'm still terrified. Some Trump supporters are openly calling for the assassination of Hillary Clinton if she wins. "I'm a patriot and it's my duty."

Several press corps holding-areas at Trump rallies are under threats of physical violence. Reporters and camera crews are scared.

A CBS reporter asked VP nominee Mike Pence if he would respect the outcome of this election. Pence said yes of course he and Trump would; but Trump isn't saying it.

Hustler magazine publisher Larry Flynt is coming out against Trump, saying he is "disgusted" with the way Trump treats women. When you're too much of a male chauvinist pig for Larry Flynt, you're in serious trouble.

CNN has been irritating me for a year with their Trump shills arguing all the time with the CNN people. Why give them so much time? Why go out of your way to have these evil people get equal say, when not one in 50 newspapers would give Trump people a free counter-page when they editorialized against Trump like a sane media outlet should?

Now I find out that CNN pays these Trump shills, like Jeffrey Lord, a good salary to take the pro-Trump position at all times. They have no room to back down if they wanted to because they are paid to argue one side. Liven up the show; keep up the ratings. Corey Lewanowski (and if I'm spelling his name wrong, good) a former manager for the Trump campaign, has a no bad-mouthing clause in his Trump severance package. In other words, he'd lose his financial base if he said a single word against Trump, and he's has been on my TV for months. I'm done with CNN for a while. They are too dominant these days. Every airport in America, every McDonalds, and every waiting room has a TV with CNN on it, whether you want it or not. They live to stir you up with breaking news 24/7.

They care more about their ratings than about trying to stop Donald Trump, and they pretend to be the leader of the band when their star anchors give Trump people the moral reprimand. For this one voter, CNN has promoted the Trump point of view more than the Trump campaign has. Now I find out that these defenders are all paid clowns, I'm pretty steamed at CNN. I was already done with Fox.

Everything I learned about the Trump Campaign's positions, I learned from CNN.

3RD AND FINAL DEBATE

Trump was nasty, rude, impossibly stupid, loud, dishonest and deplorable during the entire 3rd debate. Near the end, when she slipped in a little dig about his personal finances, he puckered up for a big pre-loaded interruption. "What a nasty woman."

You insult people at the pace of a machine gun, but if anyone fires back, they are "nasty." You're 30 times nastier than all the other politicians I've ever seen in my lifetime combined, if you exclude Alan Keyes.

But the headlines tomorrow (I shut the TV off an hour ago) will surely be his shocking answer to the moderators' question: "Will you respect the results of the election?"

"I'll wait and see. I'll have to look at it." Three times Chris Wallace made him repeat this shocking position, and like Judas, who denied Christ three times, Trump denied America and all the freedom it stands for, three times. He repeatedly said he would not abide by the decision of the voters. "I'll keep you in suspense," he arrogantly said. The man is mentally ill and playing with our lives.

This is pre-meditated treason. He is trying to incite violence if he loses the election, and he is going to lose, big time. His ego won't be able to handle it.

Tonight he again said that, "No one respects women more than I do." Correction. Everyone respects women more than you do.

He said, "I can do more for blacks and Hispanics than you can do in ten lifetimes." With that one, I burst out laughing long and hard,

Every time she pointed out something he has said or done that is on film or audio tape, he interrupts on his microphone with "wrong" "wrong" "wrong" "wrong." I'd say a nine year old is running for president but that would be an insult to all nine year olds. Seriously. The man is mentally ill and a lot of very famous and respected people are also saying this. My views are not extreme.

I heard one CNN commentator, a Republican, say, "Donald Trump is not only not fit to be President, he is not fit to be a human being."

He lies compulsively; and the more extreme the lie the better. Many times during this last debate, his train of thought was just comically contrived and all over the road.

Hillary Clinton had a few moments when she was on the defensive, but most of the time she was poised and great. You read that right. I did say great. She is the knight in shining armor right now, carrying the torch of goodness against this monstrous force of pure evil. I could easily write a ten page essay going after her negatives. I'm not interested in anything but being her friend right now, because she is certainly mine.

Mike Pence is meanwhile saying "Of course we will honor the results of the election." Well if the top of the ticket won't then you both won't. You can't honor it without him.

Now as for debate moderator Chris Wallace, what a disappointment he was last night. Donald Trump bullied him and intimidated him.

I've never liked Chris Wallace. The son of Mike Wallace went after Ronald Reagan for 8 years in a very unfair and biased way. He was always the liberal sniper. He attacked Reagan before he interviewed him, while he interviewed him, and after he interviewed him. It was a vendetta. He never responded when Reagan tried to act nice, and always pushed hard on him, interrupting Reagan over and over, almost intimidating him, taking advantage of Reagan's genial nature.

Now I need Wallace to stand up to Trump and he backs down. "Just a minute!" Trump scolded, and Wallace backed down. You wimp! Where's a real tough guy like Megan Kelly when we need a tough guy? She's the only one that has taken a fearless tone into her tough questions, not just tough words. Sure, Wallace asked Trump a couple of tough questions, but it wasn't the old bulldog (tone or substance) I remember when he went after Reagan. And every time, I mean every time, there was a test of wills between the two, when Wallace was trying to assert command and Trump refused to let him, and they were almost shouting at each other to see who keeps command of the board, it was Wallace who backed down every time.

Trump intimidated him, not because Wallace has turned into a wimp but because Wallace works for Fox now, and knows who butters his bread. I wished I could have had his job for 30 minutes just to stop the debate, hold everyone in silence for a long pause and then scold Trump slowly and deliberately and spell it out that I have the right to control this debate as the moderator. Wallace had every right to stand up to Trump and every opportunity, but he chose to let Trump bully him. You weren't my guy when you went after Reagan, and you weren't my guy when you suddenly played deferential with Trump.

Then the big tough guy Wallace scolds Hillary over and over when she went on too long. "Your time is up. Your time is up! Your time is up! Your time is up!" Oh! The big tough guy! So because Hillary would never try to bully the moderator, she gets scolded by the tough guy, but every time Wallace tried to stand up to Trump, he got his purse handed to him. Wallace let himself get bullied on purpose. Not because he likes Trump, but because he likes his FOX paycheck.

The way Trump has bullied the moderator since the first Republican debate has told me all I needed to know about him right from the start. Cooper and Radatz made feeble attempts to stand up to him and failed. Wallace didn't even make an attempt.

Trump keeps saying that Hillary shouldn't even be allowed to run for president. Anyone who is 35 years of age and was born an American citizen can run for president. If you are under indictment for e-mail deletions and a trial date has been set, you can still run for president. Victor Berger was re-elected to Congress from his Milwaukee district while on trial for sedition. Eugene Debs got 3 million votes for President from prison. Trump has no intellectual ground to stand on when he says "she should not even be allowed to run for president."

In 2020 can we find a moderator with guts who will not be bullied? Maybe Judge Judy would be willing to give it a shot. I am totally serious.

How about soundproof booths where, if it's not your turn, you can't interrupt. People always comment on who keeps interrupting, but what is forgotten is how effective it sometimes is. The interrupter leaves the enemy bleeding all over the stage and the only penalty is that the next day they have to face the journalists who remark that "he kept interrupting." So? I did it. It worked. And I'll do it next time.

People keep trying to give me Bill O'Reilly history books and I just throw them away. He interrupts people more than anyone else in the history of television. I don't watch him ever for that reason. I think it's the mark of a bad person, a really bad person, and I wish we could have one presidential debate where that is simply not allowed. They can go back and forth pretty directly, and at a pretty good clip, but your mic is off and so is the camera when it isn't your time.

MY POST - 9.21

Trump today is railing because Michelle Obama once criticized Hillary (during the 2008 campaign of course) and no one is calling her out on that. Then he adds, "All she [Michelle] wants to do is campaign." Someone politely posted a video link to Michelle actually saying it and asked why this is not counting for something that she indeed said it. The reaction against Trump is large for attacking Michelle. The poster wasn't hostile in tone.

My response, which got some likes, was:

"Valid point, sir. Mostly I'd say it's because it's traditional in American politics to rip someone during an election year early on, and then leave a trail of contradictory statements that make you look like a hypocrite. Bush 1 called Reagan's plan, 'Voo-doo economics' in the heat of the primaries, then became his VP. The Dems tried to make Reagan look like a hypocrite there, but it has minimal true import. It hurts now and then a little, but never a lot. Trump is making it seem like an old video of Michelle knocking Hillary is a big gotchya moment, when at this point, it is not. You do perform a fair minded service by pointing out that she really did say it. -- There is, however, no defense against the 'charge' that all she wants to do is campaign."

What Michelle had said were words to the effect that if Hillary couldn't manager her marriage, how could she manage the country. The crowd of Obama supporters in the small venue laughed and cheered. It was a bad, home-made video, and it was supposed to be an insider ripper moment.

What's his problem with her? The First Lady of the USA is a political player and of course wants to get involved in the campaign at full tilt. What a stupid thing it is to say "All she wants to do is campaign." Plus it's a disjointed add-on to the point that she criticized Hillary back in 2008.

NOVEMBER 4 - 4 DAYS LEFT

I took plenty of time off from writing about all this insanity called an election. The man behaves more like Hitler every day. It's over the top. It's in your face. It's clear cut fascism, and now the polls have the race very close. I'm very worried. It's the end of the world if she loses.

The big news in the last month is the FBI clearly trying to swing the election for Trump. He would give them three times the power they have now, that's for sure. He'd turn the FBI into the new American Gestapo. With a motive for wanting Trump, the FBI keeps leaking new e-mails from Hillary Clinton that officially <u>may</u> have some damaging evidence in them against her. It's clear the FBI is trying to swing this election, it's all over the news, and it's obvious stuff. I was always a fan of the FBI, now I'm ashamed of it. I feel the same way about the Republican Party and they shall have my resignation as soon as my hand can write it. I am out o-u-t and shall never be back. If this is the kind of Nazi that you can ever nominate to run for President, I want nothing to do with you ever again.

One Fox newsman said, incorrectly, that these new e-mails are almost certainly going to lead to indictments of Hillary. Now he had to apologize and retract because there is no evidence that these new e-mails are any worse than the old ones or if there's anything in there at all. Meanwhile Trump is on the campaign trail yelling about how Hillary Clinton is going to be indicted soon on the basis of these new e-mails released by the FBI Director James Comey.

All the polls have the race tightening, but Trump needs to flip at least one solid blue state to win. He could be a dead heat in the popular vote.

The other story going on for three weeks is that Trump people are planning to intimidate voters under the pretext of looking out for voter fraud, which the Democrats are supposedly planning. Of all the fascist ideas. One man in North Carolina held a rifle and a Trump sign at an early local election voting line. The state and local laws allow it. The Democrats are getting scared that their voters are getting physically intimidated by the threat of Trump-Nazis. An Ohio judge today issued a court order to the Trump campaign to stop making threats against the voters of Ohio, and to cease and desist efforts to intimidate them. Folks, this is real. It is happening here. A fascist takeover of the United States of America is in the works as I write. The Trump camp plans to contest the election, and will try to put a President-elect Clinton in jail.

There also might be a revolution in the Electoral College where Trump pulls off a coup by getting electors to switch their vote, which they can do. There is a small but lethal possibility that the Electoral College formality may be more than just a formality. One elector in 1989 voted for Bentsen instead of Dukakis.

Newt Gingrich said that this election is a referendum on the rule of law. Do we have one law for little people and one law for big people? Meaning that Hillary Clinton should be in prison because some of her e-mails while Secretary of State, none with any traitorous intent; e-mails that were sent through the wrong server and later deleted. Donald Trump wants to overthrow democracy, is going on trial for three separate charges (rape, fraud and fraud) and is clearly in the hands of the Russians. He's a total traitor to his flag.

Newsweek has a cover story just out that the Russians are clearly and overtly trying to swing this election for Trump.

So we have the KKK, the FBI and the Russians all doing their best to make Donald Trump the next president.

It's total insanity that anyone likes him. A new theory is out that he is illiterate. People asked him his favorite book a while ago and he lied, 'The Bible.' When he proved he knew nothing about it he dropped that one. More recently someone asked him to name two of his favorite books and he named the two most successful ones that he wrote. Of course, he never wrote them, he just talked to a ghost writer. Once, when in a legal proceeding, and he was supposed to read something out loud, he claimed that his eyeglasses weren't working, and he dodged it.

I guess he reads with some rehearsal off the teleprompter, as all his speeches are now formal and robotic. Same vicious message but the speeches are no longer his. They are even worse. The puppeteers are even more vile than their puppet. I've definitely got some serious strains in my personal friendships over this brute, this threat to everything that is decent in this world. Thanks for ruining conservatism, you despicable scumbag.

Trump is the worst person to ever walk the soil of the United States of America.

He's got it all set up in true Nazi fashion. If I win, I win, and fascism takes over and it's "the end of the American experiment" as a New Yorker writer put it. If I lose, it's all rigged; I really won. We will fight this false coup by the Democrats! We will put Hillary in prison and overturn the results of the election. That's what a few people are worried about right now. Trump is Hitler. I thought he'd get less and less like Hitler and the months rolled on. Instead he is more and more like Hitler every week, and now every day. With the election closing in the Trump people are screaming that its rigged, that he's going to win, (?) and Hillary must go to prison now. It's all insane.

I finally saw a good Hillary ad with kids watching TV and that monster making fun of the handicapped reporter. How could Mike Pence look at Tim Kaine in the debate, shake his head disdainfully and say, "That never happened." It's right there on film, Mike. Your man is a Nazi, and you are too, for joining the ticket and backing up his lies and his hatreds.

How did this happen to me? I was a conservative all my adult life!

One thing for sure. <u>I'm not talking politics in the comment section with chumps anymore.</u> I posted something that was anti-Trump but expressed myself so reservedly and politely that some commenter just saw a few phrases and mistook me for a pro-Trump person and commented immediately, something hateful and profane, directed at me personally, that I won't repeat.

All I could think about for the rest of the night was finding that person and doing my OJ impression. That was about three weeks ago. I haven't posted anything political since. Not saying I won't. But there's more hatred and cowardice on the internet than there is outside of it. Gotta power down on the commenting. I'm not going to Walpole over an internet cockroach.[5]

Everyone's a know-it-all in the comment section. They should call it the fighting section. No one has ever stood corrected. No one backs down. It's all rude fighting. What happened to me was no big deal in the internet world. But to me it was. No one has ever said that to me before. I'd like to make a movie about a hit squad of computer geniuses who track down these cowards, knock on their door and beat them to within an inch of their lives while quoting back to them why they are being put in a hospital.

ELECTION EVE

He's done. Stick a fork in him. The FBI has announced that there are no problems with the newly released Hillary Clinton e-mails, and it stands by its July ruling that there is no criminal wrongdoing involved. Meanwhile the "people" Trump rallies literally chant, "Lock her up Lock her up!" - Thousands of people have t-shirts and signs that have her in prison garb or some such message. It's all about her deleted e-mails and that's all he talks about in his last minute campaign speech.

"Hillary belongs in jail! She is a criminal and should not even be allowed to run for president! The system is rigged." The crowds roar. He has no case! None at all! She served as Secretary of State with integrity and made a careless error. She belongs behind bars? No, you do, for fraud at Trump University, bilking people with false claims as to what help they will receive for large fees. Accusing the system as rigged if you lose in inciting sedition.

---

[5] After Election Day I left social media for six months. When I returned I made sure I never expressed a single political thought on the internet. I have not since.

The capper came yesterday when a 12 year old boy with cerebral palsy in a wheelchair was thrown out of a Trump rally. He was anti-Trump and was saying through an electronic device, "I hate Trump." The crowd chanted USA! USA! USA! as the dangerous punk got wheeled out of there.

The story was a sensation and the Democrats made the most of it. 15 hours later, the boy was in the White House posing for pictures with President Barack Obama. Trump is toast. The race had tightened to a draw in national polls when the new FBI e-mail "scandal" broke, but with a day left, the FBI has cleared Hillary (Trump is now ripping the FBI of course) and Trump is toast.

STUNNER

Donald Trump won the election. It was the ugliest night of my life. My sisters wept all night and into the morning. Everyone I know is shocked and horrified. It was a stunner. Adolph Hitler is now my president. The sky has fallen.

For a week I've said nothing. I deactivated my Facebook account. I won't talk politics in internet public anymore. I'm done with. Say it to my Facebook, spit in my face book, disgrace book, mace book, slap across the face book, two-face book. Mostly I don't want to be connected with Trump supporters and have to listen to their cocksure and wrong on everything moronic lectures in type ever again.

For two days I thought he had won the popular vote, also. When I came out of hiding (I don't and won't watch the news anymore now) and found out she had won that by 200,000 votes it was a consolation. So without the Electoral College he loses. That gives me some hope for the nation.[6]

A lot has gone on in the news since he won a few days ago, but I gave a lecture to the Nahant American Legion Post tonight on WWI at their Veterans Day Dinner. It was my debut as military historian and the presentation was well received. I'm just going to try and stay focused on my personal life and not live in Trump-world all the time.

---

[6] Her majority will end up much higher, close to 3 million!

There are riots breaking out against him and I might have wanted join them the night he won, but now I don't want to. He won. He's in, I hate him, but I can at least give him my respectful silence for a while,[7] out of respect for the office itself.

We should at least give him a chance to show what a jerk he is, what a bad president he is. Granted, Trump would have not respected the result if he had won. Liberals would have been murdered. His supporters would have slain a dozen people nationwide, easy. Now the left shouldn't compound the problem with the very hate they hate. No rioting against him. He won. Let him at least have a 100 day Honeymoon. That is the American tradition. Opponents give the new guy a 100 day chance to surprise everyone.

I'm not going to root for him to be a bad president. I hope he can improve his soul and find some decency in there. He has shown none of that quality so far. Not even decency, let alone kindness. He is a terrible man. But maybe he can do a Chester Alan Arthur and be a much better person as President than he ever was before it.

TEAM

Ed Meese? Really? I didn't know he was still alive. Trump is announcing his team of lizards, and the name of Reagan's disgraced Attorney General, Ed Meese is out there. I'm a big Reagan fan and even I had to concede that Ed Meese did great harm to Reagan's reputation.

People are freaking out all over the country about the upcoming Trump Administration. It makes me sick that I even have to type that up. For 15 months I had just prayed for the day I could put that man's obnoxious voice behind me. Now it's going to be part of reality itself.

TEARS

---

[7] 2020. He has done nothing to change my opinion of him as the worst American that ever lived. But I gave him a chance.

The word is that at 6 am, November 9, Hillary Clinton called a friend and was inconsolable. Hillary was not just crying, she was incoherent. The former First lady was sobbing and trying to get her words out.

One more reason for me to cry too. She wasn't just crying because she lost, she was crying because of who she lost to, the worst American of all time, the most vicious evil man in all of American history, and now he's my next president. The TV analysts were telling us that the Clintons are spoiled and she cried because she didn't get her spoiled brat way. No. She was crying for me. She cried for all of us. I cried for all of us.

Now a friend is sending me pro-Trump jokes in my e-mail box and I protested and he did it again and I snapped at him and then he called me closed minded and said sarcastically that "I thought you were a peace and love guy." As though Trump stands for peace and love. You sent me 8 years of racist anti-Obama memes in the e-mail and I said nothing. I make it clear that I hate Trump and asked you to stop sending me pro-Trump e-mails and I get back "I thought you stood for peace and love and were open-minded."

"Be open minded" means "agree with me." It's always meant that, it's never meant anything else, and it never is invoked when one agrees with you. No one has ever reacted to agreement with, "Now I could be wrong. Don't take my opinion as a fact. Be open minded." It is only invoked in a hostile context under the guise of suggesting fairness.

My library is too big to move it to Canada. If only I could pack light and had more money I would just move to Canada. It's a $6,000 application fee. I've been looking into it.

I hate Donald Trump. I hate Rudy Guiliani. I hate Mike Pence. I hate Jeffrey Lord. I pray that my country can survive the triumph of evil. Cause that's what this is, you know. It's the triumph of evil. I never ever hated a President before. Not one. Not even close, never even came close to hating a President, and I always took some pride in that.

My e-mailer is a fool because he represents millions of Trump supporters to me. I was drifting towards acceptance, reconciliation, and open-mindedness until you sent me these hateful rub it in your face things.

One was a 'meme' that has Obama and Bill Clinton whispering to each other that they actually voted for Trump. When am I supposed to laugh? I protested and he comes back with a link to a Sean Hannity article with the headline "Toughen it Up You Crybabies - Donald Trump is Your Next President!"

This is your idea of accepting that I don't want any more pro-Trump material?

I have read almost zero about this hideous situation since the morning he was elected by a minority vote with the help of the Electoral College.

As November dies down and the votes are all carefully counted, Hillary Clinton's popular vote majority increases. It is now 2.2 million votes. She won the popular vote by 1.7%, an acceptable margin of victory in most countries without an Electoral College rip-off system. Not since 1824, when Jax lost to John Quincy Adams, has a candidate won by that large of a losing percentage. This fact will be in the news quite a bit for the next 4 years, I suspect.

I have not been watching the news AT ALL, and had to look this one stat up out of curiosity. The next thing I want to look up is which state she won by the highest percentage, and that's where I will live.

NOVEMBER 27, 2016

The Trump goon squad is forming up. There is talk of making Rudy Giuliani the Secretary of State. Just shoot me! (Rudy might just do that.) There is also talk of making Mitt Romney the Secretary of State. Trump loyalists are furious. Romney attacked Trump early on and tried to stop him from getting the nomination. Now they might ask him to be Secretary of State?

Just like during the campaign, we have the bizarre picture of Trump spokespersons on TV arguing against the very line that Trump is putting out. Trump is not denying that Romney is under consideration. I would favor such a move. That would show me some character. If Trump puts unity ahead of revenge it would be an encouraging sign. Giuliani is despicable to me, and Romney I like.

Trump is now claiming that millions of people voted illegally in California and Virginia and that's why he lost the "so-called popular vote," as he puts it. Why is it so-called, dummy? That's what it is, that's what it's always been called, and the term is 1,000% accurate, so what's with the "so-called" popular vote? You moron!

Every news agency and fact-checking agency is reporting that Trump has provided not one shred of evidence to back up the charge at all, let alone substantiate it.

On the other end, the Green Party has raised $4 million in two days to organize a careful re-count in Wisconsin, and then, maybe, Michigan, and Pennsylvania.

If anyone could rig an election, it would be Trump, with Russian help. If the Green re-count proves Trump innocent, it will have done him a favor. If it proves that the fraud committed fraud in Wisconsin, it might mean civil unrest over who retains power.

Please, let it be Romney. He can temper Trump, or at least he won't make trouble with his temper, as Giuliani might. A Romney Secretary of State would show that Trump does not want to surround himself with yes men.

Trump's yes women are on CNN all the time. They are suddenly giants in Washington and they're awful. All of them.

NOVEMBER 30, 2016

Trump recently reacted to a flag burning incident with this Tweet - "That guy need to be put in jail for burning the flag! We have to deport anyone who burns the flag!"

Trump set fire to, in two sentences, two important parts of the United States Constitution and legal system. In 1989 the Supreme Court ruled that is it not against any law to burn the United States flag. I would say that Trump has no respect for that decision, but the obvious truth is that he obviously has no idea that the Court made that decision. As for part 2, the United States cannot expel a citizen for having a hatred for the flag. You have to practically try to overthrow the government to get expelled from the USA. I tried it twice, and I'm still here. Trump shows, once again, that he is a shallow ignoramus when it comes to anything to do with technical matters. He reacts to things like a self-righteous drunk at the ball game who is sure the umpires are all on the take. When his team wins, he admits they are honest umpires, but when his team loses his is absolutely sure there is something fishy going on; and he is so low, deep down, that he isn't even posturing. He's sure of it! He can't even laugh at himself and see, even for one rare moment, the prejudice and hypocrisy in his track record.

DECEMBER 22, 2016

I don't watch the news. From what I've heard, he may hold the Inauguration at the Trump Hotel in NYC instead of in Washington, and he plans to continue on as the star of the TV show, *The Apprentice*. The USA had never had more of an apprentice in the White House.

Romney is not on the Trump team as of now, and probably was never really being considered. Maybe Trump just used the prospect of Romney in the cabinet to gain image-points as a uniter and a forgiver. And then he just doesn't do it.

This could be the end of us all. When I hear that Moscow is being evacuated, I'm heading to the roof of my building with a jug of wine.

I know that he hired Texan Rick Perry to be his energy secretary, and Ben Carson to be his HUD man.

In the final popular vote, Hillary Clinton has now won by almost 3 million votes.

Meanwhile, the stock market had jumped 8 percent in one month due to the so-called Trump effect.

They know the score. Don's going to stick it to the little guy while the big guys laugh out loud like drunken pirates. It makes sense that Wall Street likes him.

XMAS MORNING

For Secretary of State, Trump has named Rex Tillerson. I've never heard of him. Rex is the president of Exxon-Mobil, and has ties to Valdimir Putin. The country is sold out. Exxon Mobil's gas prices are always inexplicably higher than any other gas station. T-Rex is its president and he is in charge of American foreign policy.

DECEMBER 28, 2016

Trump is complaining that the media doesn't give him enough credit for the charitable donations he has made. That's a laugh. He's fighting with everyone, and he isn't even in yet. We're in the eye of the hurricane.

Protest marches against Don's election accomplish nothing. He won, okay? She beat him by 3 million votes, but he won.

I hear that she blamed Obama, in part, for her defeat. Barry didn't support her until too late. Possibly; but does she remember that at the 2008 DNC, she shocked everyone by making a speech that notoriously lacked any words of praise or support for him? I had forgotten about that until recently. Not one pundit failed to note the obvious insult to Obama in her 2008 praise-less speech. Obama didn't pay her back deliberately, but it was payback time, nevertheless.

NEW YEAR'S EVE 2016

As for Trump, I stand by everything I wrote about the man and the candidate during the election, but I have no intention of trying to hate him, now that he is my president. Some hatred of him will happen, I'm sure, but my default position is that I swear to you I am going to try and respect him, try and give him the benefit of the doubt. Even if I don't respect him personally, I at least owe it to my country to try and respect the office of the President of the United States.

I was unhappy when Obama first became President, and he turned out okay.

Re-reading this chapter, and all the terrorist attacks, and how I felt about them all, well maybe this jerk is the man we need to go take care of business against these scumbags who set girls on fire because they won't be sex slaves. Reviewing my feelings when he first ran, and how I at first liked him, I can try and reach back and find some consolation that someone who favored a strong foreign policy, as opposed to a Democratic one, is now coming in. The problem of course, is his recklessness and stupidity. I have to hope that he is now surrounded by a lot more smart and responsible people than he was in the fall of 2015, when he was acting like the nastiest impossible spoiled child in the School for Brats.

About three days ago he was talking about Israel and some controversy, the details of which escape me. He was talking very-pro Israel, quite the opposite of a few things he said during one of the debates that upset me, as seeming not pro-Israel at all. The few moments I saw I liked. It wasn't just what he said, it was the way he was saying it. He seemed to have a serious presidential tone. It wasn't his words; it was all the little things in his voice, his eyes and his body-language.

I have to try and hope. I don't want to focus on negative attack energy. It's bad for me. I think I see the change in him that people were hoping they would see after he became the nominee, and did not.

Becoming the nominee gave him his own crowd to play to only; but this time, for the first time, he can't play only to his supporters, and I think he gets that point! That's a huge plus if he does. How can he not? He may not like having to tone the little boy wild man down, but it looks like he understands that he is obliged to.

I posted something on Facebook about him on Election Night, where I actually tried to see the good in him. There wasn't much, but I tried to. I was posting on the presumption that he was going to lose, so there was no need to hate him anymore.

When he won it was the worst night ever. I deactivated my Facebook account on November 8.

A professor in California called Trump some awful things last week and had to leave the school. Not because she was expelled, suspended or fired, but because she got so many death threats on Facebook and Twitter that she feared for her life. Trump Nazis will physically hurt you if you criticize him. The Gestapo is on the loose now.

The point, being, social media is an open door to a storm of hatred that wants to come into your home. I realized, after a while, that most days that I am upset, it's because of something someone wrote to me or about me on Facebook.

A friend of mine, who can hold his liquor, calls New Year's Eve, "Amateur Night." Facebook is Amateur Night for writers and I've wasted a lot of writing on Facebook trying to be a good sport and a friend to all, and then all I get back is smart-ass wise-cracks, and condescending lectures from people who are stupid and think the reverse is true.

I will write a hand-written letter of support to Obama before he leaves office.

NEW YEAR ATTACKS BEGIN

One hour after midnight in Istanbul, two Islamic radicals dressed as Santa Claus shot up the *Reina* nightclub, killing more than 41 people.

They are going out of their way to attack festive gatherings to maximize the impact and reaction.

Now I see the big movie coming out about the Boston Marathon, with famous stars doing the best atrocious excuse for a Boston accent. Making a big movie like this encourages terrorists to keep up the bad work. I've seen the big promo where Donnie Wahlberg says, "They messed with the wrong city."

Please.

JANUARY 10, 2017

Another 'terrorist' attack, this time at the Ft. Lauderdale airport. Some nut came out of a men's room and shot five tourists to death.

Trump and his henchmen keep trying to explain to everyone that they aren't racist. Meryl Streep at the Golden Globe Awards used her acceptance speech to not accept the upcoming Trump presidency. She went on about him instead of talking about her film career. All these awards ceremonies are no longer about the awards, but about who makes the controversial political play. Trump fired back at Streep on Twitter, I don't recall his insult. I could care less about the Golden Globes or what Meryl Streep thinks about anything.

The Democrats, led by Schumer of NY are planning strategies on how "to stop Trump." He already won.

JANUARY 12, 2017

Recent news: Trump first press conference as President-elect went about as badly as can be expected. He responded to a tough question by CNN reporter Acosta with, "Your organization is terrible. You're fake news."

Some at FOX thought that was great and I won't quote them. But Shep Smith at FOX too the high ground and said, "It is our [his show's team] observation that CNN's correspondents followed journalistic standards, and that neither they, nor any other journalists should be subject to belittling & delegitimizing by the President of the United States."

A report from Buzzfeed was critical of his relations with Russia and he answered with, "Buzzfeed is a failing piece of garbage."

Meanwhile his nominees for Secretary of State and Defense are appearing before Congressional committees and contradicting virtually all of Trump's stated positions on controversial issues! There's never been anything like it. Mattis at Defense and Tillerson at State are speaking out against the border wall, and against banning Muslims. They talk of accepting the Iran nuclear deal and declaring NATO inviolable. The man who appointed them doesn't seem to agree with one damn thing they say! Trump is going to have to run the country with a Lincoln majority on everything: Its nine against one, looks like the one has it unanimously.

JOHN LEWIS

John L. Lewis is a famous old black civil rights icon and congressman. Very Dem and very left. JLL said on January 13 that he will probably not attend the Donald Trump Inaugural because his election was "not legitimate," meaning the Russians interfered and got him elected. Trump Tweeted back at Lewis to look out after all the crime in his own back yard, plus a few other typical barbs.

That's the latest. He's reaching out to be everyone's president by insulting the most revered black man in the US government besides President Obama.

There have been a couple of lone-wolf terrorist attacks in the last few days. When are we going to start calling them "crime sprees," instead of the flattering term, "terrorist attack?" Charlie Hebdo and a loser at a shopping mall in Peoria are two different things.

LAST DAY OF PEACE

He takes over tomorrow. Today is the last day of peace and I just wrote President Obama a hand-written letter of support for his 8 years in office.

Trump spoke up about devaluing the dollar, and half the Wall Street gains of the Trump-bump disappeared overnight. The public disapproves overall about how he has handled his transition. According to the Wall Street Journal, his initial momentum after victory is already falling off, and even some of his supporters are grumbling - this when he isn't even in office yet.

I told Obama, in my letter that I just mailed, that he was a good person, a fine man and a great president. I also told him that I didn't vote for him, but almost did in 2008.

NOTES: The following was written within a few weeks of his taking office.

OUR NEW LEADER - 2017

If not for the Russians, Trump NEVER WOULD HAVE WON! He is a pawn of the enemy of the USA, Russia. The Kremlin OWNS HIM.

He is a bully and a disgrace to humanity.

I liked Trump for a month when he began his campaign, but a month later I hated him. With each passing day I came to hate him more. It never ends. He is my president now and he gets worse every day.

Trump does have one redeeming quality: He can't live forever. He is an over the top racist, an infantile narcissist and he inherited his money. Trump is a bully and a liar, a thug and a liar, a sexist and a liar, a braggart and a liar, and a fascist and a liar. Other than that, he's awesome.

The night he was elected, a man walked down my street screaming "He needs to die!!!" Nothing like that ever happened in anyplace I have ever lived. Within 50 days in office he has declared all the major media outlets to be "the enemy of the people" and he is going to do something about it. He has accused President Obama of tapping his phone during the campaign, offering no proof yet calling Obama "Bad (or sick)!" Look who's talking!

BIO

Prologue: A boy of six years of age has been warned to "Stay away from the Trumps." Why this warning? The Trumps were sadistic bullies and Mom says, avoid them.

One day the Mom left the boy in a playpen on a warm day in the back yard. Next thing you know the boy is cowering before an assault by an older boy named Donald Trump. "He was using my playpen for target practice, just throwing rocks at me for no reason. Took his time, too."

This is from a biography of Trump by a Washington Post reporter. This is the man that my fellow Americans somehow elected to the Presidency of the United States. There aren't any stories like that from the childhood of any other American President. George Washington is famous for throwing rocks across a river that no one else had ever managed before (or since!). He certainly wasn't throwing rocks at a smaller child in a playpen.

My country has elected an out and out mentally ill sociopath to lead it. God help us survive this horrible man! He is the last person on earth I would want as my president.

He was born in Queens on June 14, 1946.

Trump had an older brother named Freddie who "died of alcoholism." Donald Trump never drank or smoked and says that this event was why. Freddie died of a heart attack at 42. I guess it can be called death from alcoholism, but technically, it was a heart attack. He had become an airline pilot for TWA. Freddie was like Joe Kennedy Jr. in that when he died, the younger brother walked onto the pathway to the presidency.

The key to Trump is probably the trauma of being sent to military school in the 8th grade as punishment. Fred Trump caught young Don with a switchblade among his possessions and punished him by taking him away from all his friends and his home. An already defiant angry boy went from bad to worse. That would ruin a good kid let alone someone who threw rocks at little children in their playpens.

Trump's grandfather ran some brothels in the old Northwest. He had left Germany to avoid the draft, came back when he was too old to serve. He was deported back to America because they knew exactly what he had done and didn't like it.

Fred Trump had to pay a large fine for racial discrimination in his NYC housing units

Mary Trump, the president's mom, was born in Scotland, and was far from rich. She came to America and married Fred. Mary had a big crazy high orange colored hairdo, and Trump obviously emulates her with his version, and it's kind of creepy really.

Trump went to Fordham, and then to Wharton College, a part of the University of Pennsylvania system. He got out of the Vietnam War by claiming to have a bone spur.

Trump is famous for his world-wide business empire, and for one word: "bankruptcy."

One investigative reporter studied Trump's life and came to the conclusion that the only thing he ever clearly succeeded in was his 11 year run on a TV show as on-camera talent. He was the star of NBC's mean-spirited reality show, *The Apprentice* from 2004 to 2015.

Before he won the presidency with Russian aid, Trump had failed at everything. He was the King of Bankruptcy. I'd hear his name and think, 'Oh, the bankrupt guy.' I played craps at a few of his casinos when I played in Atlantic City.

I intend to get copies of all my books shipped to someone who lives in the middle of nowhere so that they survive the nuclear war.

Donald Trump is the end of America and maybe the end of the world.

He is the worst person in all of American History, let alone the worst person elected President.

During the presidential debates, Donald Trump was rude to everyone in a most shocking way. No such level of persistent immature brazen discourtesy has ever been part of a single presidential debate. But with him in it, all of them were like that. He is the rudest man ever to debate for president.

Can you imagine how liberals feel about him if this conservative feels this way? I don't like the lefty protesters; I like conservatives as my default position. But this guy, how in God's name did we elect a demon?

God, how I hope he gets impeached or dies from a heart attack. 95% of all the people I know HATE HIS GUTS FAR MORE THAN I DO! And listen to me! 5% love him. He needs to die, he really does, and Pence and Giuliani can jump in the fat coffin with him.

INAUGURATION 2017

This was the saddest day in all of American History.

Within hours of finishing his rotten speech, the no good jerk fired every US Ambassador and ordered them home immediately. Power ego trip jerk has to "fire" everyone the first chance he gets. Now he can't run his transitional days and weeks effectively. No one has ever come into office on such a hateful arbitrary power-tripping note.

The big headlines on Jan 21 are about Ivanka Trump's biography on her website. Seems that she was liberal enough on LGBT, climate change and a few other controversial items, and on the day of the Inauguration her new bio takes that all out. Her jewelry business is now the main focus.

CIA AND CROWD SIZE

In less than 48 hours, Trump announced that he is "having a running feud with the media." "And these are some the most dishonest people you ever want to meet. Believe me."

Like your White House Press Spokesperson who lied about the crowd at the Inauguration.

The media showed the crowd size from air photography comparing Obama's First Inaugural to Trump's and proving that Obama's crowd was much bigger, and it was (no one that I knew, watched the 2017 Inaugural on TV - nobody.) So the Trumpeter comes out and explains that this is a media lie. Then he adds two lies as to why it APPEARED that the crowd size was bigger with Obama. News outlets broke down the statements as outright lies.

He's been in office 48 hours and he and his spokespersons have told more outrageous lies than any previous president told in his entire term.

On day 2 in office, Trump gave a speech in front of the CIA memorial to fallen members. He has been accused of being highly critical of the CIA in the past.

Trump said:

"There is no one, no one, more strongly supportive of the CIA than Donald Trump. No one. No one."

When he says this self adoring, and inarticulate statement, the audience cheers, but you never see them on camera. That's because he packed the room with supporters who cheered on cue, and meanwhile, most of the CIA veterans were standing there with folded arms and stern faces.

The news outlets rolled out the tape later on of him viciously criticizing the CIA activities: "These type of things happened in Nazi, Germany, okay?"

Well then, it's okay to make Nazi analogies. Once he does it, with regard to a patriotic American organization, the rest of us can do it.

Trump is a Nazi! He isn't technically a Nazi but the things he says and does, these type of things happened in Nazi Germany, okay?

FRESHMAN SENATORS

Here are three of the seven new Senators who were sworn in on January 3, 2017:

Nevada - Catherine Cortez Masto - Democrat

Illinois - Tammy Duckworth - Democrat

California - Kamala Harris - Democrat

New Hampshire - Maggie Hassan - Democrat

John Kennedy - Louisiana - Republican

Maryland - Chris Van Hollen - Democrat

Indiana - Todd Young - Republican

Tammy Duckworth is a veteran who lost two legs in Afghanistan.

THE WALL

Trump is arguing with the President of Mexico about "the wall" and the arrangements for their upcoming meeting on January 31. Now Trump is Tweeting that maybe the President of Mexico should consider the 31st a free date. Trump is playing thug businessman, threatening to cancel the meeting.

The President of Mexico insists that he is not going to pay for the wall, and Trump is insisting that he will pay for the wall.

The President of Mexico addressed the Mexican people and finished by saying that Mexico offers and expects respect from the new President. Sad how he's obviously worried that he and Mexico won't get any.

WALL THEM OUT

He made if official on January 27. No more immigrants from Syria until the USA develops a more thoroughly cruel vetting process. He made good on his promise to be a bigot if elected. He is not disappointing his followers.

Meanwhile every Trump hater has to come up with a new USELESS conceited way to "protest." Two young men scaled a skyscraper to unfurl a banner hating Trump and when arrested they make a pompous speech about how they are doin something noble. It was all just personal self-aggrandizement under the guise of protest.

CHAOS AT THE AIRPORTS

The dictator placed a ban on entry into the USA against six Muslim countries near the end of January. It was without warning, as well as without precedent. Thousands of immigrants at airports were stranded with no home to immigrate to.

Demonstrations against Trump's racist move erupted all across the country.

Copley Square in Boston had thousands of demonstrators against Trump.

It is a nightmare.

The Mayor of Boston is speaking out against and feuding with Trump. Twitters wars are aflame all about.

TRUMP FIRES ATTORNEY GENERAL YATES

The acting Attorney General, Sally Yates, refused to implement Trump's executive order barring immigration from 6 countries, so he fired her.

Massive public demonstrations against Trump are commonplace, and he hasn't been in office two weeks.

DT has nominated Neil Gorsuch to be the next Justice of the United States Supreme Court. He is 49 and very conservative.

FEB 4, 2017 - SUPER BOWL EVE

Rex-T has been confirmed. The big oil companies own America, just like the lefties have been warning us about all along.

Now a judge in the State of Washington is blocking President Trump's travel ban on Muslims in several countries, citing personal endangerment of these individuals by the sudden implementation of the measure. I'm fairly sure the Washington judge is not challenging Trump's right to make the move, just how he's making it.

Almost every talk show in America is yapping about it, and the country seems divided, which is sad, because it should be 9-1 against this fascist move; but then again, he did win the election, so this shouldn't surprise.

Trump fans are happy because their man delivers. He promised he would be a fascist racist thug when he ran for president, and now that he's in, he 'gettin it done.' He tossed some personal insults at the Washington judge, for no reason at all. He keeps tweeting insults at the media, lumping them all into one basket with his ever grandiose statements.

It's the campaign trail all over again. Trump says things that are patently untrue. The media calls him on it, saying that he has no evidence, and they have plenty to prove him wrong, then he attacks the media.

In a way, though, I'm happy to see the country in a tizzy about the Muslim travel ban. It means that the world is not on the verge of a nuclear war with Russia. As long as I do not hear the dreaded words, "we have unconfirmed reports coming in now from CBS News that Moscow and Beijing are being evacuated," I'll deal with the Donald Chump insanity stories all right (I hope.)

Here's a 900 page biography of Donald Trump, abridged into two words: He's evil.

WARREN SILENCED - BATTLE OVER A SO-CALLED JUDGE IN SEATTLE

It is pathetic when the President of the United States refers to a judge who rules against him as a "so-called judge."

That's what Trump tweeted about the Washington judge, James L. Robart, who is blocking Trump's travel ban on six Muslim countries. That fight is all over the courts. Trump's Supreme Court nominee, Neil Gorsuch told Senator Blumenthal of Connecticut that Trump's tweets were "demoralizing and disheartening." Sid told Neil, "They are a whole lot more than disheartening."

What a horrible man.

I watched Jake Tapper trying to confront Kelly Conway on Trump's many shocking lies, while she tried to smile and change the subject with campaign rhetoric. Trump claimed that there had been an overall 47% spike in the national murder rate over the past four years and when Tapper told Conway this was a total lie, she said, "Does that mean we are supposed to ignore all the good he is doing for this country right now?"

In the Senate, Elizabeth Warren (D) was giving a speech opposing the nomination of Jeff Sessions (R) of Alabama for Attorney General, when Mitch McConnell (R) of Kentucky interrupted her and asked the chair to invoke an ancient rule about impugning the motives of a House member. After some back and forth, the chair ruled in MM's favor and a shocked Elizabeth Warren had to sit down. This was big news, and now the spin seems to be that since she was reading the words of

Coretta Scott King at the time, the move backfires on the Republicans. I do not agree. I think it was a humiliating moment for Warren and that she's had it coming for a long time with her angry tirades. All she knows how to do it attack. I enjoyed seeing her silenced.

Supposedly she got her big revenge by making speeches on the internet, but that looked humiliating to me, also, adding self-insult to her injury.

(If Trump can call a judge 'so-called', I can say that Donald J. Trump is a so-called human being.)

FEB 11 - ROBARTS

Three are new concerns over the safety of all U.S. judges now that Trump has decided to insult any who don't agree with him, just like in the election campaign.

James Robart, the Washington judge who is blocking Trump's travel ban on Muslims, is getting all kinds of death threats on sociopath-media. Judges are corresponding with each other all over the country expressing concern for the safety of all judges.

White House Spokesliar Sean Spicer said that Trump has no regrets about what he said about Judge Robart.

Meanwhile a former British spy is getting a lot if ink about a Russian dossier on Trump they had compiled when he was visiting there over the years as a businessman. They supposedly used it to blackmail him during the Election Campaign, which would explain why he was praising Putin while the U.S. Congress was expressing outrage at Russian behavior.

We're all still here!

FEBRUARY 13, 2017

National Security Advisor Mike Flynn is in trouble over revelations that he was making phone calls to the Russians about U.S. policy before Obama left office. It is a breach of several laws and many people are saying that Flynn should step down.

Meanwhile Trump keeps bringing up this lie about him being the victim of mass voter fraud. He's singling out New Hampshire where thousands of outside the state voters were supposedly bused in to vote Hillary. Politicians, journalists and citizens from all over New Hampshire are uniting to say there is zero evidence to support this and we all had our eyes wide open that day.

I'm with journalist Andrew Sullivan who believes it is time for the media to start questioning the mental health of Donald Trump. I've felt that way since I watched him behave like a six year old during the 2015 Republican debates.

Estimates or the cost of the wall with Mexico are in the 100 billion dollar range.

FEBRUARY 16, 2017

The press conference of February 16 was mostly this lunatic we elected president railing on about how dishonest the media is. My friend Susan says, "He's going down."

In less than one month he has reached Richard Nixon levels of scandal, with his close advisors in cahoots with the Russians. It's so obvious that his supporters in redneckland can only try to defend him by saying that a U.S.-Russian alliance is a good thing. They don't even dare try to say that he wasn't working with the Russians to try to rig - excuse me, influence - the Election of 2016.

Russian spy ships are patrolling off the East Coast and that hasn't happened since the Cold War supposedly ended.

At today's press conference Trump talked about North Korea and paused with an evil happy gleam in his eye to note, "We're going to take care of things there, folks."

It clearly looked to me like there are plans in the works to finish the Korean War for General MacArthur. My nephew, Andy C., just got sent to Korea as a tank driver. It looked like Trump knew this was going to happen and he knew that wheels are already turning.

FEBRUARY 18, 2016

Trumps war with the media and everything else has him in a Nixon 1974 mode, and he's only been in office 28 days.

John McCain is giving speeches in Munich to America's allies disowning everything Trump says and does. McCain held back during the Election campaign, but now he's furious, and who isn't? Who with a decent bone in his or her body isn't furious that this liar is in the White House? I'm disgusted that he has happened and I hope he falls.

It's not a good scene when the articles in the papers defending him read things like:

NEVER MIND TRUMP'S MENTAL HEALTH - WORRY ABOUT OUR COUNTRY

These headlines are common. Those who dislike him are simply overtly questioning Trump's mental health. I say there is no health there to question. He is mentally gone. He showed it during the entire campaign. This is just a continuation and now the stakes are world peace and the American Way.

Trump's ass-kisser Bill O'Reilly (FOX) asked him the other day about how he is palsy with Putin. Bill asked Don if he had misgivings about getting along so great with a killer. Here is Trump's response:

"There are a lot of killers. Well, do you think our country is so innocent?"

Good God in heaven, what weak, sick, infantile logic is that? It's the same as during the campaign: Change the subject with a specious attacking counter-point or an insane reframing of the issue.

The Senate is getting in gear to find out just how far Trump is in deep with the Russians. I hope it leads to impeachment and I hope Trump drinks a bottle of sleeping pills.

THE CAMPAIGN RALLY OF FEBRUARY 19, 2017

I wrote during the Campaign of 2016 that for Trump, the campaign rallies were not a means to an end, they were the end itself. It's what his ego needed and wanted, and if he won, fine, if he lost, not so bad either, as long as he keeps getting these fixes for a year or two.

Now, with everyone in agreement that his first month in office is "a disaster, just disaster folks, just awful, disaster, really, a disaster," Trump flies to a rally in Florida that has the press mystified. It is exactly like one of his campaign rallies in October 2016. Everyone can't even understand it. The election is over. You won. Everything is going wrong. You call the media horrible names and say they're all out to get you. Third-rate names are turning down posts in your administration. Your solution: Go to Naples Florida, appear before a cheering crowd and make all the hateful statements you made during the campaign, while wearing one of your stupid, 30 years too old for a man your age caps, and say absolutely nothing useful to your situation. As a bonus you also get the chance to put your stupid foot in your mouth.

"Look what's happening last night in Sweden."

There a conflict on tense, so it's bad English, plus there is nothing going on in Sweden!"

This is the second time in three days he's made public assertions about a terrorist crisis going on in Sweden, and the world is laughing at him. Newspaper headlines all over the world were already mocking him for Tweeting about a crisis in Sweden that did not exist, and then he goes to a campaign rally a month after he's elected and talks about the crisis in Sweden yet again. This man is completely insane! I've followed politics for 50 years and I've never seen a campaign rally a month after an election. It was exactly like a rally with a week to go, not something like. Totally bizarre and a lot of pundits felt the same way I do. What on earth is the point of this rally when you have work to do as president? Are you trying to campaign-rally your ratings up? Looks to me like that's the only explanation possible.

I've tried to watch his insane 1st press conference three times, but it's hard. He is such a turn-off. The so-called president stops in his opening fake speech to boast for about three minutes about how remarkably well he did in the Electoral College! My God, how transparently shallow can you be? "Folks, that was the biggest margin of victory in the Electoral College since Ronald Reagan." Pathetic. No one in history has ever bragged about how well they did, specifically, in the Electoral College. It's over the top insanity, right off the bat. More important, he is obviously playing super-sleaze-bag in dodging the trillion-ton fact that he lost the popular vote by the largest margin ever for a winning candidate.

[The constant campaign rallies never stopped until no one even thought it odd anymore — Only C-19 stopped them — They sure seemed odd at first, following victory, before he made it normal.]

GOLF BE WITH YOU

Trump ripped into Obama on Twitter for years, the twit, for golfing too much. "Obama golfs over and over and over and over," wrote Trump in his usual Dikensian style, back in 2015. Trump Twit poured it on during the Election Campaign about Obama golfing. "If I were President, I'd want to stay in the White House all the time and work my ass off," he posted.

Two days before the Election, Trump the twit Tweeted against golfing O that "Golf is fine, but always play with leaders of countries and people that can help up!"

Cut ahead to February 20, 2017. Trump has been President for 30 days and has now gone off on private golfing trips six times! His aide-liars keep denying that he is golfing or they say it was only a few quick holes when it was 36. Don is not golfing with foreign leaders. He doesn't want his skull clubbed in.

The press has finally shown proof to the Trump spokes-fools, and now they are back-tracking and admitting that Trump is 'gone fishin.' When asked if this makes Trump a hypocrite, the Trumpeters do the usual change-the-subject and attack-the-press duet.

Trump and his team are inveterate liars about all matters, great and small.

Trump never back-tracks on how he plans to take the oil of Iraq, "next time we get the chance" (wink.) Yet Defense Secretary Mattis said in Europe that "we are not in Asia to seize anyone's oil." Maybe he has to get fired soon.

Someone else on the Trump team got fired the other day for including one criticism of Trump in a 90 minute speech that otherwise praised him. You'd have a better chance of surviving as a Red General in Russia under Stalin in the 1930's than as a Trump official for four years.

If the monster: the beast, lasts that long.

CNN DEBATES - ?

I'm doing my history writing all through the night and over my shoulder I have the TV on with the sound off. I keep seeing these clips of the debates.

Scrolls about the debates. People arguing about who won the debates. Teasers before the commercial break about new debate stories.

It first I thought it was an historic look at the 2016 Presidential Debates. Then I see it's the "Democratic Debates."

The campaign is over. What the hell is going on here?

After two hours of copy-editing a JFK book, I had to go over and see what this was. Were there some Democratic governor's races up for special election?

Who are these people debating like Trump and Rubio on national television, and what on earth are they debating about. What are their goals?

Finally I stopped and paid attention. They are all unknowns and they are debating for who will be elected as chairman of the DNC! Are you kidding me? CNN is running a prime time debate, and treating it EXACTLY LIKE - not something like - a November Presidential Election debate - and all it is, is to see who gets elected by Democrats to be their chairman.

Bogus and Lame.

CNN is just looking to make money. Keep ratings up. Can't lose those hot ratings we get during real election years, lets create election years when there aren't any.

Since when does the job of head of the DNC merit a nationally televised debate with 8 candidates going through all the motions of a presidential debate? That's the biggest pile of bull I have EVER seen!

Most American do not know or care who is the chairman of the DNC or the RNC. There are much bigger news stories going on, and CNN knows it. But it also knows that the public loves fighting and arguing. People can't drive past a car crash on the other side of the highway without slowing down and that's the cash CNN cow.

So CNN just creates a political football to kick around and use for an excuse to hold a hot, feisty debate. The immoderators analyze who won, while ignoring the much larger question: who cares? These people are all unknown names and we are supposed to get all worked up about who wins? No, we are supposed to get all worked up watching them get worked up. That's the appeal: the arguing; the yelling; the interrupting; the rudeness; and the sound-byte where someone unleashes a vicious, witty zinger. That's what it's all about.

Not the job they are campaigning for or the issues they are arguing about. CNN knows how the machine works; now it has to find meat to throw into it.

There aren't any real elections. Our ratings are slipping. Let's solve this by inventing an election crisis that does not exist.

All TV drama is based on arguing. It's 85% of all dialogue and the other 14% is out and out violence. 1% is people being nice to each other. That's the TV drama pie. Turn on any 1 hour TV drama and test my pie. It's all arguing. That's what sells. Maybe they aren't raising their voice, but all the characters are at war with each other, even lovers and friends and family. It's all about disagreement; and that's all it's ever been about, all the way back to *Gunmoke*.

So political shows and stations know the rules, too. They have to contrive argument or else they slip and fall by the wayside.

That's how CNN elected Trump. They gave his spokesliars a zillion hours of free air time because it stirred up ratings to see them arguing with the CNN people. [On the other hand CNN never criticized Trump during the campaign unless there was a Trump defender on the panel. That was incredibly commendable, even if it contributed to the disaster. And all the more reason the president shouldn't bemoan how unfair CNN is to him. During the campaign, CNN was incredibly fair to him.]

FAKE NEWS

He keeps calling the media the 'fake news.' Look who's talking. The biggest liar of all time.

"This dishonest press! The fake news is the enemy of the people!" I saw him virtually yell all this, so I add the exclamation marks. "The fake news doesn't tell the truth! It doesn't represent the people! We're going to do something about it!"

How fascist can you get?

That's so much like Nazi rhetoric it's honestly frightening. The first people put in the concentration camps in Germany were the left-wing journalists and intellectuals.

Now the idiot is having a "feud with the FBI." Of all the foolish things he can do with his power, a top one would be making an enemy out of your best weapons. He's throwing his ruby slippers into the sea in the first scene. One month in office and he is making the people at the water cooler at FBI headquarters start to hate his guts. That's really stupid on his part and great news for all the good people in the country. Now the FBI will be less likely to help him with his plans for fascism in America.

Here's the feud. The Trump team is in trouble for alleged illegal contacts with the Russians before he was inaugurated. The Trump team issued denials and then pressured the FBI to back up those denials. The FBI flatly refuses to back up Trump teams' denials. Trump strikes back like an infant. He Twitter-attacks the FBI about leaks to the media that the FBI is failing to stop. It's not even a direct reaction to the FBI's refusal to back him up on Russia. It's just an animal scratching at your face. In this case he is arousing another powerful animal in the FBI. Good for him. Good work Don. He insults everyone everywhere he goes. He is a disgrace. He is my president.

For the first time in my memory the President will not attend the White House Press Corps Dinner. It's the annual classy event where everyone shows up in a spirit of fun. The Press sorts of roasts the President with jokes, he laughs along, and at the end gets everyone back. Obama knocked it out of the park, and was genuinely funny. I know two comedians who have performed at it. Trump has announced he will not attend. Of course not. He has made an open enemy of the press, he can't take the most microscopic criticism without wigging out, and he is a mean and evil man in every way. Of course he will not be attending the dinner. I was already imagining that he could not possibly attend, and he can't. He has no choice. He cannot attend because he cannot attend, period. It would be "a disaster, believe me folks, a disaster, a disaster, unlike anything you have seen in decades and decades and decades, believe me, decades."

SPEECH TO CONGRESS

His first speech to Congress was obviously written by his puppeteers. It was full of reconciliation and unity and I had to shut it off. Every time he is being mean he is being himself, every time he is saying reasonable things, he is obviously reading words he did not write OR THINK.

Nothing will ever get me to stop hating his guts.

He mentioned the recent Kansas City shootings and says we all must condemn hate. A man walked into a bar in Kansas City and picked out some foreigners for death. He screamed "Get the hell out of my country!" and shot two men from India to death who weren't even Muslims. Everyone I know said "That's the kind of atmosphere Trump's hateful rhetoric has created. Some people blame Trump directly for the Kansas City shootings. I do too.

STOCKS SOAR

On March 1, 2017, the Stock Market jumped to 21,000, up 300 points in one day after Trump's speech to Congress. People are talking about how great it was because he didn't insult anyone or stir up trouble.

HE DIDN'T WRITE A DAMN WORD OF IT, WHO'S KIDDING WHO!

SESSIONS

AG Jeff Sessions has recused himself from the case involving him talking to the Russians when Trump was President-elect.

Now Sessions is saying that he only made small talk with them, nothing of importance, but he therefore had lied during the Senate hearings when he said he hadn't talked to them at all.

He is so far to the right on everything that I have no pity of him at all. He is an extremist, the most right wing senator of them all.

Trump is standing by him amid calls for him to resign. Senator Schumer is leading the way. Sessions should resign, says Charles.

16 Dems signed a letter saying he should resign.

I knew this would all come back to haunt Trump - I thought so during the election when few people were denying that these Russian connections were going on, but all anyone really cared about was who won: Hillary or Trump, we'll deal with these rumors later. Later is here. This is so much fun to watch. The Presidency is the sun in the solar system of hate and criticism and you're not dishing it out any more. Now you can stand there and take it. You can threaten back all you want, but you're just a big blowhard.

OBAMA IS A SICK GUY

I'd give anything to see Trump fall into a well.

I HAVE LOST ALL RESPECT FOR THE OFFICE OF PRESIDENT OF THE UNITED STATES. This is ruinous to my serenity.

Now he's Tweeting an outrageous <u>unsubstantiated</u> accusation that President Obama had Trump's phone tapped. He said "How low can he go, tapping my phone. He is a bad (or sick) guy!"

As always with this knave, there is no evidence to support this.

The President of the United States is a liar. Simple as that. The news analysts have reached a point where they offer amused explanations that we are now just used him saying things that have no basis in fact.

In other words the President of the United States is a lair.

Now he's mad as Jeff Sessions for recusing himself from the Russia investigation.

And he keeps insisting "If Vladimir Putin likes Donald Trump I consider that as asset, not a liability." That makes one of us.

He wants the Russia thing to go away. He's angry because that news story is dominating his first two months in office.

He is such a relentless jerk all the time, day after day, that we get past the point of debating politics and we just want get a chance to smash his face in.

Trump is the worst American citizen ever. He is a tireless Canadian cold front, ruining the tone of everything.

Don, make America great again: kill yourself.

THE ENEMY OF THE PEOPLE IS NOT THE NEWS MEDIA, IT'S DONALD TRUMP

The Orange bum Tweeted this one:

'The FAKE NEWS media (the failing New York Times - NBC News - ABC News - CBS News, CNN) is not my enemy, it is the enemy of the American people!'

Truer words have always been spoken.

How can he get away with such over the top Nazi talk and threats? How did anyone vote for this sack of garbage? He is the worst person ever to inhabit America and he is trying to deport undesirables who commit crimes illegally. If you want to deport undesirables, start with yourself!

Trump is a liar, a cheat, a bully, a racist, and a traitor. Mostly he is a liar. He lies all the time all day and night. Don lies in his dreams.

Why doesn't Obama sue him for libel for claiming that Barack tapped his phone during the campaign?

All of his spokespeople are liars too. They know they are lying. Sean Spicer lies all day for Trump.

He is the most thin skinned jack-ass that ever lived and he's my president? I would pay to watch 40 liberal teen-aged girls kick his ass for, oh, about an hour … hour and a half.

You might think this extreme BUT I TALK TO PEOPLE ALL THE TIME WHO FEEL THE SAME WAY. They usually have ther own unique and creative visions of how they would like to see him harmed. And it's never quick.

Here's another orange gem from a recent speech. Since some presidents have had disputes with the media, his 20,000 times too extreme position is therefore justified:

"Thomas Jefferson, Andrew Jackson, and Abraham Lincoln, and many of our greatest presidents fought with the media and called them out oftentimes on their lies [not true with Lincoln - only subversion of rights, not on lies] . *When the media lies to people, I will never ever let them get away with it. I will do whatever I can so they don't get away with it."*

You and your vague threats; your infantile language. What exactly are you going to do, you lying pig? You suck beyond all human definition. He is evil and the world is in great danger with him in control of the nuclear weapons.

John McCain is a conservative and he is fighting you on this one. Chris Wallace is on the attack (we needed him to stand up to him during the debate) saying, "Trump has crossed the line now!"

Yeah, no kidding Chris. Trump has declared all the major news outlets to be the enemy of the people. The media is the friend of the people. I would never want to meet him and have to shake hands with him.

MARCH 11

John McCain is calling on Trump to either retract the accusation that Obama tapped his phone or show some proof. Trump ignores.

Saturday Night Live is the number one internet news story for its vicious spoof of daughter Ivanka Trump's new cologne called "Complicit."

In Trump's White House, Ivanka playing the First Lady and virtual White House Chief of Staff.

The Washington Post is calling Sean Spicer the worst Press Secretary of all time. His lies are becoming almost a yawn. The Post could have added "in any country."

The big story is a US District Court Judge out of Southern New York who was reported to have resigned. The Judge tweeted that "I did not resign, I was fired!"

Trump and Jeff Himmler have been pressuring the Obama District court judges to resign, and most of them have. The laws are vague; and custom rules the waves on resigning and hiring District judges with new administrations. Occasionally an appointment will be retained throughout the successor's term, and there isn't usually a great rush to get the old people out, but Trump is bad, so he is pushing the Obama judges out a little too fast in the case of the SDNY judge. That story is all over CNN.

US TROOPS GO TO SYRIA

He's finally done it. In the second week in March 2017, US troops have gone to Syria to get involved in that civil war. On March 11, 125 soldiers went in to solve a crisis that is 2,000 years old. On March 13, DT announced that 400 more were going in to join the fight for the city of Raqqa. ISIS says that their capital is Raqqa. Taking it means they will move elsewhere, not that ISIS will fold. But I'm not saying I'm opposed to this either. I lean to no because you're risking a clash with the Russians and there aren't any real great sides to be on over there. On the other hand, the only reason I liked Trump for the first month he was running for President in 2015 was that he was promising that he would do something about ISIS including putting boots on the ground. He was critical of Obama passivity over ISIS and I was with him on that. Then he started offending me 86 trillion times, but that's another story. So now he's doing what I sort of wanted him to do but now I'm recoiling because Syria is too close to sparks with the Russians. He's claiming that he is fighting ISIS with the Russians not in competition like a cold war confrontation by proxy.

This is how the USA got into the Vietnam War, in tiny increments and then one big commitment. Two different situations, I know, but it's still got a scary Nam in 1962 feel to it with JFK sending over a few more "advisors." The 500 Rangers in Syria are a serious little pop. President Assad is making angry speeches insulting America as having lost all the wars it gets itself into from Korea to Iraq, and saying that American troops are invaders who will only end up humiliated.

PATHETIC LIAR ROCKS ON

After 11 days of silence on the trumped up charge that President Obama tapped Trumps' phones at Trump Tower during the campaign, the jerk has spoken.

"There are a lot of definitions to what constitutes wiretapping, and I think over the next few weeks you are going to see some very interesting things come out. Very interesting things."

In others words, you're full of it. You reign through the stupidity of 48% of the electorate in a contest you lost by 3 million votes, and you are spinning the same tactics you used as a businessman. My quote is paraphrased, and if you look it up you'll see that I was kind, and it's even more transparent windbag all over the road delay, confuse, obfuscate jive than I wrote it up as! I was paraphrasing kindly! Bigly!

Even square interviewers with bow ties who have led conservative talk shows for 20 years are asking him to please come up with some proof or retract these criminal allegations against Obama. Does the ass hole even know how serious these charges are? Democrats on the Intelligence Committee now have to divert attention from their investigation into the Russia ties and put them instead on this wild goose chase based on the Twit's Tweets.

One Representative on CNN said that the whole 'Obama tapped my phones' business is nothing but a clever attempt by Trump to deliberately distract the investigative process and the media from the real threat to his power, the Russia connections; you know the ones, the ones that pythons like Rush Limbaugh laugh off as "ridiculous!" "Not a shred of evidence to support these outlandish almost comical accusations!" - No Rush, there's tons of evidence you fat big mouth one-way boor whose presence on earth hurts humanity. You can SAY stuff ALL YOU WANT with your BIG FAT MOUTH, you and all your kind. But it doesn't make you right.

Don, how dare you accuse President Obama of tapping your phones! How dare you call him "sad" or "sick!" - Look in the mirror you lunatic weirdo with the bad doo. You and Rush are diseases with legs. You two jerks ruining America with all your right wing hatred.

Trumps keep referring to all the media as the Fake News. Then he lies and lies and lies and lies, and then Kelly Ann Conway lies for him and lies and lies and lies and lies and then Sean Spicer spices up their lies with more lies of his own.

Sean and Kelly keep insisting that "people are simply taking his Tweets too literally. He is new at this business of being a politician, don't forget that."

On both counts: are you kidding me? You're still using the old campaign excuse that he's new at this? - His Tweets are loud and clear and not the least bit vague. Four different Tweets: President Obama tapped my phone. There is no literal vs. figurative issue in play here. "Obama tapped my phones! He is either a bad or a sick guy!" is not up for argument or interpretation. Now he's splitting orange hairs over the definition or a wiretap. No Jose, everyone knows exactly what a wiretap is, you tapped drip.

In a related story, rapper Snoop Dog has made a music video which has a clown pop up behind him that looks exactly like Donald Trump and Snoop shoots the clown down.

Trump and his spokesgoons are very upset about this. Trump Tweeted that this video is disrespectful and if anyone made a video like that about Obama, it would have meant "Jail time!"

Well yeah, you make a valid point on that double-standard, but look at your own double-standard. Snoop says it's just figurative art, and you say no. Then you say that the former President tapped your phones, offer no proof and you don't think that's disrespectful, or flirting with "Jail time!"

The best epilogue is Trump Lawyer Mike Cohen saying this exact quote:

"I am very disappointed in Snoop Dog. I thought he was better than that."

That is hilarious. Say it ain't so Snoop! You usually set such a high standard for decency.

MARCH 17, 2017

The outrageous charge of tapping his phones won't go away. Leaders of both parties continue to call on Mr. big mouth to show some proof. Meanwhile the White House dragged the British intelligence community into it. One of Trump's liars said that Obama had approached the British secret service with the request to tap Trump's phones. The British intelligence service almost never makes any public official comments about anything, and went bananas with denials that it had any connections with the American election campaign in any way. The White House had to make an official apology to the British government.

"But Putin's a killer."

Trump: "We have all kinds of killers. What, do you think America is so innocent?"

He just makes that stupid stare when O'Reilly dared to play real interrogator and then says something stupid he can't get out of later.

The stock market continues to love him. I continue to hate him. I talked to Barry Crimmins and he mentioned something about the Inaugural speech and I said I hadn't seen it.

"Wow! Even you! Nobody I know watched it! Not one person!"

Since he told me that I've asked around and no one I know watched it. I've watched most Inaugurals in my lifetime, I didn't even think to turn the TV on that day. Virtually everyone I know seems to have felt the same way.

Trump also Tweeted that *"All negative polling is fake news."* Italics mine: Unreal. That was his opening sentence on a Tweet. Any polls that do not favor his administration are fake. Trump deserves to be keelhauled.

He and his liars keep insisting that "Wiretapping covers a lot of different things. Obviously he didn't mean it literally and it wasn't directed at Obama personally."

No. Wiretapping only covers wiretapping; you spelled it out literally four times; and you made the accusation very specifically against Obama personally. You horrible person. "I think you're going to see some very interesting things come out over the next few weeks." Hopefully your brains after you fall out a 14th story window.

MERKLE

The sober drunk President met with the German Chancellor that he insulted on social and mainstream media during his campaign for office. There he stood next to Angela Merkle. During the 2016 campaign he said that if she is elected "The German people will probably overthrow her." and more recently said she "is the person who is ruining Germany." Now he has to stand beside her and smile and say what an honor it is to be with her today.

The reporters keep asking him about his criminal accusations against Obama for tapping his phones. Trump jokes that they two of them actually may have something in common. I guess there really was some evidence that US intel had tapped her phones years ago, but the joke distracts from the important point that no one actually did tap his phone; so the joke got a ripple of a laugh, but it makes no sense. How can you have something in common when noone tapped your phone and you're just a liar about it?

Sean Spicer's saying London had something to do with it, and Trump is defending him saying that it's something that "a very talented lawyer said on FOX News so you should be talking to Fox News." FOX News is denying any such reporting, but Media Matters shows lawyer Neopolitano or however you spell his name, saying this very thing in an interview. Trump and Spicer are twin-rats for extrapolating one moment of a statement on one TV show into a giant crucial and factual story, but FOX is dodging the responsibility of their right wing guest making the misleading statement in the first place.

"I think you are going to see some very interesting things come out in the next few weeks." Yeah, more and more relentless instances of you using vague false assertions.

Now they're calling his new healthcare system "Trumpcare."

What an oxymoron.

North Korea now has 12 nuclear warheads but does not have the means to deliver them.

OBAMACARE WILL STAY

Trump promised during his campaign for dictator of a democracy that "The first thing I will do is repeal Obamacare. It has been a disaster."

He calls everything a disaster. The cliché riddled dip. He sucks beyond belief. I digress. So late in March, the Republicans withdrew their replacement plan from a House vote because they knew they didn't have the votes to pass it.

The health care system of Obama will remain, and headlines all over the country talk of this major defeat for Trump and his party. I am not knowledgeable about these heath care plans and have no favorite. This is like Hillary Clinton when her big First Lady health care package reached the Congress in 1993-4 and got voted down. I remember the analysts saying that the problem for Clinton was that he had called in so many favors to get this one passed, that it was a double whammy that it did not. A little bit the same here. Plus he can't handle any wounds to his pride.

Ted Koppel told Sean Hannity to his face that Fox News is bad for America. "Does that include me? Am I bad for America, Ted?"

"Yes."

Hannity's response was, "Well that's really sad. Really really sad." Well, Sean that's really really true.

It's not sad, it's right on the money. You suck for electing Trump. And you did. If there's no Hannity, there's no President Trump. Hannity was keeping Trump up when no one else would have him on TV at his lowest point in the 2016 campaign (after the grab them by the pussy stuff.) I hate Hannity like I hate migraines. Right wing reactionary is always validating right wing lies and claiming that all left wing accusations are "ludicrous." You are bad for America. And you are not well-read. You're just a fucking big-mouth. 30 years in radio and you're written two fluffy essay books.

Alan Combs died last month and Sean gave all these holy memorial tributes to him. They used to have a radio and TV show together, but Hannity couldn't stand having Combs disagree with him so he fired him. Then he dies and all of a sudden I'm supposed to get teary eyed by your tributes to Alan. You tried to have a show where people were allowed to disagree with you, in this case a guy you couldn't intimidate, and you couldn't hack it. I used to watch that show because you had to defend yourself against someone who wasn't intimidated by your interrupting, but you couldn't take it. Combs had to go, and when he dies 11 years later the hit man shows up with the flowers. I would never go on your show. Not that I've been invited, but I know four of five comedians who have been on FOX political shows and I could push to try and get on there. I have one guy in particular who has been on and can get me an interview to get on a show or two. I'm not interested because I feel that FOX is right wing fascism and full of lies. It's a dishonest network. The president promotes FOX TV shows on Twitter! And he says that CNN is unfair and biased.

And I want the opposition press to stop saying "Five Pinnochio points" and "pants of fire" and "he says things that aren't true." Get to the point! Donald Trump is a goddamned LIAR!

APRIL 3, 2017

A lot has happened in a month. The latest is that Steve Bannon is finally in some trouble and might have to step down as Trump's Harry Hopkins.

My favorite current story is that FOX's Bill O'Reilly is being exposed as an (alleged) sexual harasser around the FOX studios. Good. I hate that bully big mouth conceited heartless dummy. He gets all high and mighty putting down a black rapper because his lyrics are "demeaning to women" but now it's revealed that FOX has had to pay out millions to settle several sexual harassment lawsuits against him at FOX.

There's some other FOX people involved in this sexual harassment business, it's an interlocking grid of ass grabbers. Sponsors are pulling ads from his show.

He and his network are a disgrace to everything that is fair and decent in this world. Not that I love the Rachel Maddow lefty crusaders either, but O'Reilly is probably the second worst right wing media person alive after that fat disgusting lying rat, Rush Limbaugh.

O'Reilly the bully interrupter will survive, but I'm enjoying the agony he must be feeling right now as a nationally disgraced bad person. Ha ha ha ha ha ha ha!

APRIL 7, 2017 - TRUMP USES THE TOMAHAWK

Donald Trump didn't like the video images of Syrian children who were dead or dying from Assad's chemical attack.

He was upset by these images of little babies dying.

So he broke out the guns and ordered the Navy to action. Ships in the Mediterranean sent 59 Tomahawk Cruise Missiles to strike Shayrat Air Base, in Syria. At least five more Syrian children were killed in the attack. So Trump answers the death of innocent children by killing more innocent children in response.

Having said that, I guess I liked it. I hate to say it, but I liked it. Russia was furious and condemned Trump and America. Assad was furious and condemned Trump and America.

This was a lot different than a drone attack on a home somewhere sheltering Yemeni terrorists; this was an attack on the Syrian Air Force and the government of Syria.

I've heard a lot of criticism for this action, but none of it runs deep. It seems that there is always a way to spin it and rip Trump in the process, but if Obama had done it, the Dems would have applauded.

It does help Trump against the charge that he is in too deep with Putin and Russia.

Many people criticized the Navy because they only destroyed buildings and planes, and didn't try to crater the runway. Why didn't they try to crater the runway?

In 1942, the Japanese used to shell tiny Henderson Field on Guadalcanal for six hours with heavy cruisers all during the night. They made the runway look like moonscape. By 11 am the next morning, Hendu was back in action again. It isn't that hard to fill holes and then smooth them out. A bunch of drunks can do it for minimum wage. That's why the US Navy didn't concentrate on cratering the runway, you dummies.

HE WON'T SURVIVE

I thought he would but no, FOX fired Bill O'Reilly in mid-April. For 20 years he bullied people on the air and that's why I hated him. I hate bullies. All he ever did was interrupt and intimidate with his skilled use of the great power of the spoken word. Intimidating someone in an argument doesn't make you intellectually right. It just means you know how to intimidate someone with the tricks of the verbal trade. Only late on his career did O'Reilly start to write serious history books with the help of a giant staff. His earlier books were just the same rants that he said on TV, except in print.

The other stations had two days worth of headlines, while FOX News led off with a story about Trump rallying to revive his new health care proposals. They surely addressed it, but with a short hit and run. Every time I peeked in on FOX, when the whole world was talking about the king of right wing TV hate, they were talking about some story no one else was interested in except FOX. A century from now O'Reilly may be forgotten, but he is the biggest news story in the world right now. I liked a few of his commentaries over the years, but he personally became so revolting that I completely stopped watching him about two years ago. The idea that he was being illegally touchy feely with women and verbally insulting makes perfect sense, based on watching his behavior on the boob tube. I do not think that O'Reilly is remotely brilliant. He thinks he is. I know someone who worked with him at Channel 5 and he off-handedly mentioned that "We of course all knew that he wasn't the smartest guy in the building, and we were surprised to see him become the big political star." The person who told me that was an on-air personality, not the floor-sweeper.

I met O'Reilly once at a Stitches Comedy Club show. Backstage, he told me and Barry Crimmins a racist joke about an Indian girl. Crimmins faked a laugh, O'Reilly laughed at his own joke and he walked away. It wasn't funny, besides being racist. Barry and I just looked at each other and shared a knowing laugh.

[June 2020: It's so great that he's been gone so long now. Yahooooo! Now if we can only get rid of the nasty blonde bitch.]

GORSICH CONFIRMED BY NUCLEAR VOTE

After more than a year with a Supreme Court of only 8 members, the United States Senate finally confirmed the Trump choice of 49 year old conservative, Neil Gorsich. The vote was 55-45 and only three Democrats voted for Gorsich.

On April 22, a new poll showed Trump's approval after 100 days to be 42%, the lowest of the last 13 Presidents; the lowest at this point in office since those polls began. His core support base has held strong, however, which makes sense. They turned out to vote at twice the rate of their opponent.

Now even the stock market is having second thoughts about Trump and is leveling off after some euphoric gains in his first weeks in power.

MAY 7, 2017

On May 4 there was a big protest demonstration in New York City against Donald Trump. They even didn't have a specific gripe; it was a just a few thousand unemployed people protesting Mr. Trump's coming home to New York. A few weeks earlier it was millions demonstrating that he must release his tax returns. It's getting to be a bit contrived. There's a big national protest march scheduled for June, demanding answers to the charges of collusion with the Russians during the 2016 Election campaign. Some people are already working on that for the opposition. Blocking traffic in 16 cities won't solve anything.

I let off plenty of steam about him in this book, and I hate the guy, but the people who oppose him need to stop adoring themselves for being so morally superior. Maybe he is a bad person, but that doesn't mean you're a good person because you protest. What have you done lately to make a difference?

One woman had to be taken off an airplane because she refused to sit next to a man with a Trump T-shirt on and she loudly demanded a new seat while lecturing him about Trump. She was escorted off the plane while people of both parties applauded. Every other music band has a song ripping Trump. I get it, but you are making no difference at all with this type of behavior.

The late night talk shows are unwatchable. I hate Trump, too, but I tuned in to see a variety show, not a lecture from young lefties. Entertainment suffers when polemicists with props try to make that combo work. I get it. You have morals and you care.

So Trump can't go to his own Tower in NYC and had to get out of town. He explained that he didn't want to cause any more disruptions in New York, so he cut his visit home short: to a half a day instead of a few days.

What's it like to have a tribe? I forgot the feeling.

[2019 update – The pro-Trump rallies go on and on, but the initial burst of mass anti-Trump protests has slowed down and vanished somewhere along the way.]

MAY 8, 2017

Sally Yates and James Clapper dominated the headlines of May 8, as they testified before Congress about possible ties between the Trump team and the Russians. Yates testified that she warned president-elect Trump that Michael Flynn was vulnerable to Russian blackmail, and was making illegal contact with Russians.

For two days before the hearing, Trump was Tweeting about Yates and her upcoming testimony, coming on strong with his opinions. CNN reporter King and others are appalled and are saying that as students of the law, they feel that this is witness intimidation; and coming from the President of the United States.

During the Yates hearing Trump kept Tweeting about "Fake News!" Now even a Senate Investigative hearing is fake news. The Obama administration now admits that it warned Trump about Flynn two months before Yates did. Trump keeps Tweeting that this is just old news, but all the networks (besides FOX of course) are saying that some of this testimony is indeed new.

MAY 10/11

President Trump fired FBI Director James Comey and things are really heating up. Just when Comey is closing in on Trump in the Russia investigation, he fires him, with the help of the Attorney General who has already recused himself from any participation in the Russia investigation because he is personally connected with people involved.

On May 11, Trump met with top Russians at the White House AND THE FREE PRESS WAS NOT ALLOWED IN.

It's getting scary.

The initial White House stated reason why Trump fired Comey is that the new Deputy FBI had studied Comey's record and had been appalled at how cruelly he had prosecuted Hillary Clinton over the e-mail scandal of 2016. Trump is all broken up about how mean Comey was to Hillary last fall.

Trump had praised Comey for going after Hillary and led crowds in chants of "Lock her up! Lock her up!" Now he's upset because Comey wasn't fair to her and that's why he fired him!

Good grief! Trump is evil, transparent and pathetic.

Comey found out he was fired while he was giving a talk to Los Angeles FBI Officers. It came on the TV and he had to end the speech. Low class Trump as always. No guts, either.

All who know him say the man with the "you're fired" act is the last person in the world that wants to fire anyone in person.

Every non-FOX commentator I have seen is disgusted and concerned that this is bordering on an attempt at a complete crushing of the rule of law and its replacement by the rule of fascist right wing regime.

Huckabee's daughter is deputy White House spokesliar and she has no business being on camera. She is total nepotism and an unsure public speaker. She makes Carly Fiona look like a supermodel.

Trump is claiming that the whole Russia thing is simmering down, that he has been cleared of any wrongdoing three times by Comey (unsubstantiated and everyone doubts it) and that his firing has nothing to do with the Russia investigation.

Former Nixon speechwriter and ubiquitous TV talking head David Gergen even gasped a sarcastic "aw!" when a commentator said that Trump insists that the Comey firing has nothing to do with Russia.

A few weeks ago Comey was testifying and Trump was Tweeting live in real time during the hearings. Comey kept saying that yes, Trump is under active investigation, while Trump tweets, "See? Comey just said I am completely not under any indictment. I am totally in the clear."

This kind of rank Trump stupidity went on all afternoon.

So Trump was just Tweet-acting. He really was fuming, and on May 11 a couple of people whispered to real reporters that the moment Trump lost it and decided to fire Comey was that day a month earlier when Comey told the world that Trump was under investigation over Russia. He was waiting for the right moment to do it, and with the Congress starting up a lot of investigative programs, and the heat getting close, Trump decided to fire Comey.

MAY 19, 2017

So much has happened in the last ten days. Wow! People are starting to use the I-word and use it casually: IMPEACHMENT!

Witnesses inside the government are slowly coming forward to spread the truth about just how far our new "president" will go to spit on the American Flag and all it stands for.

When Trump had a meeting with the two top Russians, the Foreign Minister and the Ambassador, he had the meeting alone. They chummed it up for cameras in private, and it's OBVIOUS that he is over the top selling out the country to them. They laugh and smile and their talks are private and even many Republicans are sickened by it.

Four days ago the *Washington Post* headlined that Trump had revealed classified information to the Russians at that meeting which might hurt America's ability to fight ISIS, and these claims come from inside the government.

The latest is that he told the two Russians that "I fired James Comey because he was crazy. A real nut job." Trump has even said point blank now, admitted now, that he fired Comey to relieve the pressure of the Russian investigation. He had work to do with the Russians and the investigation was getting in the way!

So you see, in order to keep making deals with Russia while all Americans are excluded from the meeting at the White House, he had to fire the FBI Director because he was putting too much pressure on him. Please don't investigate my potential corrupt ties with Russia; for heaven's sake I'm trying to make a secret deal with them in the Oval Office. That investigation might interfere with the deal!

Trump is so used to strong-arming and bullying everyone over the course of a coarse lifetime that he can't change his habits and now it's just getting him into trouble. He's way over his hideous head and he doesn't get how strong the forces are lining up against a corrupt president. You aren't going to get away with it! You can't bully the FBI! You can't intimidate the American press with nasty Tweets you scum.

When are all these rube rednecks going to realize that this man is not your friend? He is selling your country out to America's enemy, Russia, you dumbasses with your threatening bumper stickers. Your guy is the most un-American man in America. He is a traitor.

He hasn't been in office six months and he can't get anything done and has made a total jerk out of himself.

What I suspected, what we all did about that secret meeting with Comey at the White House, was true.

Trump asked Comey to quash the investigation on his potential corrupt activities.

OBSTRUCTION OF JUSTICE

Trump made veiled threats to Comey on Twitter about how he had better watch what he says on Capitol Hill because "our phone conversations may have been recorded."

Trump asked Comey to pledge his personal loyalty to him, and when Comey gave a clearly evasive response, Trump became angry. He wants a loyalty oath to a person, not to law or American principles.

These last two items: asking Comey to quash the investigation point blank, and his demand for personal loyalty, are what really has set off the I-word, and properly so. He's in treacherous territory now. The scenes of him meeting with the Russians, while the three of them are mocking and laughing at the FBI Director as a nut job are enough to make me wish for worse than impeachment.

Right at this moment, for the first time, I feel there might be a threat to his core support. If this traitor business, (and he is definitely an American traitor) keeps coming on strong, some of the redneck right might start to drop off. He's got this core 40% support of dolts that don't care what he does. They never change. Keep hammering away at those people. One of these days some real redneck leaders are going to step up and say, "We make a mistake supporting this viper!" Then it will all be over.

There's a small but strong group of Republican leaders who are very much against him. When that group gets up to 25%, he's done.

Meanwhile, in other news, Roger Ailes, the founder of FOX News, fell down a flight of stairs in his home and died at the age of 77. He tripped over a Bill O'Reilly book, *Killing Ailes*.

It's so beautiful to hear all this talk about impeachment. So beautiful. DT has never been able to implement a single goal. All he does is swat the flies away from all the horrible stinking baggage he arrived with.

The United States Congress and the American Press are in universal agreement that Russia meddled in the 2016 Presidential Election. Even some people who like Trump admit that. Then he gets in and has secret meetings at the White House with the Russians, the American press isn't allowed in, no US Congresspersons are allowed in, and he calls the FBI Director names after firing him while the three of them laugh.

Ambassador Lavrov made a mistake when he made a sarcastic joke at the press.

The USA was all upset about the Comey firing. Trump is laughing it up with the Russians behind closed doors, and when they came out to face reporters for 3 minutes someone asked Lavorv is the Comey firing will have any effect on negotiations.

Lavrov countered "Really? He was fired? You're kidding me!"

Some analysts thought maybe he didn't know. It was so vicious and sarcastic. Lavorv and Trump are in cahoots against Comey and against the American Press. To disrespect an American reporter like that in the White House, well, nothing like that has ever happened before.

Many people besides me are beside themselves with rage and disgust. The last ten days has seen a total sea change.

I see a real possibility of impeachment proceedings before the 2017 World Series begins.

The FBI does not hire "nut jobs" as its Director.

Trump is so stupid he never understood that befriending the FBI is the key to power, not insulting its leadership.

Basically he fired the FBI director over Russian allegations and then he high-fived the Russians over it.

Comey is starting to break his silence.

The first time Comey met Trump was at a big formal occasion at the White House and Trump pointed him out from the far side of the room. Comey had to cross the crowded room. Comey reached out to shake Trumps hand (and admitted he was already uncomfortable with being singled out like this, plus Trump made a stupid wisecrack) and Trump pulled him in and forced a big hug on him. Trump was showing the world how buddy-buddy they were and Comey was appalled.

The FBI does not appoint crazy people to head the department, you complete ass hole. What a defense! The FBI is closing in on me! What should I do! Fire the director and call him a nut job.

Stock markets all over the world took a tumble because the impeachment talk is clearly serious!

I will drink champagne when he is impeached!

MAY 30

Last couple of weeks the heat get hotter on Trump and the Russians. One Connecticut Representative had the greatest speech in which he said that Trump attacks every group on earth at home and abroad, except the Russians.

Facebook had a picture that said:

Like or share if you've never said the words,

"President Trump."

Wow. I hadn't made a conscious decision, but no, I have never said it. I may have written it once or twice, but I won't say it.

Jared the Son in Law is under FBI investigation now.

Trump just wrapped up his first foreign badwill trip, stopping first in Saudi Arabia.

PARIS CLIMATE ACCORDS - MANCHESTER BOMB

The USA has pulled out of the Paris Climate Accords. Only Nicaragua and Syria are with Trump on this one.

In Manchester England, on May 22, a suicide dork blew himself up at a rock concert in the name of Islam, killing 23 people, many of them children. The rock star was a female singer I have never heard of named Ariana Grande. Many more were wounded badly. He thinks he pleased Allah, but he did not

KATHY GRIFFIN

For a whole week now, it's all anyone wants to talk about. Kathy Griffin this, Kathy Griffin that. "What's your take on what Kathi Griffin did, give us a call."

I have confessed this to no one and I confess it here for the first time: I have no idea who she is.

Apparently she's a famous comedienne, I don't know what she does, but she did a photo-shoot where she held up the bloody, severed head of Donald Trump.

Outrage! One caller is so offended; the other yells, "You hypocrites, what about what Ted Nugent did with Obama?" And on and on.

Who cares? What a tempest in a teacup. What counts is whether Trump is in cahoots with the Russians (and it's the only thing that adds up from the way he behaves.)

Kathi is making apology videos. Bill Maher is making apology videos because he dropped the n-word during an interview, thinking it was a hip joke, but it came out ugly. You bunch of wimps. And I don't care what these comedians think. Truly they never add anything useful, and "incidents" like these usually help their careers. Every day some comedian is in trouble for something they said about politics and it's all over the news. People ask me for my take on it. You wanna know my take on it? I have a house full of books written by advanced thinkers and I don't waste time on flat superficial observations from comics who just want attention.

SESSIONS BACKING OUT

June 7: Now Attorney General Jeff Sessions is reportedly bickering with Trump and has offered to resign!

Comey is going to testify before the Senate tomorrow and it's the biggest TV suspense show since the day of the OJ verdict. The word is that Comey was upset by what Trump said to him about killing the FBI investigation into Trump and Mike Flynn, and told Sessions, "Don't ever leave me alone with him again. Tell him how to communicate with me through proper channels."

Trump was clever enough to make his exact words to JC vague, so I don't see this leading to an impeachment, but a lot of people feel that it's heading that way.

In any case, Trump can't work on any of his agenda if he has one. All he can do is fend off the scandals. Now even Russia is admitting that some Russians did hack the American computer system in order to try and influence the election towards Trump against the Democrats. Putin says it was the work of private citizens he had no control over … so now they are at least admitting it.

Meanwhile you have people like Limbaugh still high-pitched screaming into the radio mic that "all this Russia tried to influence the election business is utter nonsense!"

Because you said so?

The entire legal system is blocking Trump's attempt at blocking Muslims from entering the country. He is not exactly making America great again at this point.

COMEY TESTIFIES - JUNE 8, 2017

FBI Director James Comey testified before Congress. It was one of the biggest national TV events ever.

The Republican Senators who questioned Comey were disgusting. They were like some nasty lawyer in a movie who is fighting for an unjust verdict. What reaches they employed. One jerk from Missouri asked him in a nasty tone, "So you were disturbed by the President's behavior, yet you continued to show up for work every day, is that correct?"

What a reach!

If you were hoping that Comey would go easy on Trump, you were out of luck. He kept his poise and chose his words carefully, but he hit the mob boss with all guns blazing.

Comey said up front that he had to take memos at the time because he was nearly sure that Trump would lie about the encounter. He didn't say the word 'liar' but he used the word 'lie' several times. "Given the nature of this individual," he had to take notes.

This big question was: where would he come down on whether Trump saying "I hope you can see your way to letting this go. Flynn is a good guy" was an attempt at coercion. I was shocked at how bluntly he said it was clearly an attempt at coercion.

Comey was clearly personally hurt by being fired, and the way it was done. He said he was fired because he hadn't played ball the Trumps way. He said that Trump was obviously implying that if he wanted to keep his job, the president expected to "get something in return."

The Republicans disgracefully tried to make minor points, major ones, or played word games. Rubio's questions made it seem as if Trump was merely asking for "loyalty" as a general quality, not as in being part of a cover up. Nice try, slick. McCain attacked Hillary Clinton instead of Trump, his lowest moment in a long career in which I have always disliked him or hated him, depending on the year. It was all about how we have such a double standard with how we are going after Trump compared to Hillary.

First of all, she isn't the president, okay turkeys? Second, Trump is betraying the country to the Russians, and she made a mistake with her e-mail server. The opposite is true. The double standard is how rough you Republicans are on Hillary and how you look the other way no matter what Trump does.

LORDY

That's the word of the day in the aftermath of the big Comey testimony.

Lordy, I've never used that word before until this sentence.

Back on May 12, Trump had tweeted that Comey had better watch what he says when he testifies because there may be tapes of those conversations.

Firstly it implies that Trump is taping private conversations without the persons knowing it, in the White House. Second of all it is a threat against the FBI Director.

When asked about the matter of the tapes Tweet, Comey said, "Lordy, I hope there ARE tapes."

That says it all. He's not the least bit afraid of the big bully, and he knows what was said.

The Republican Senators who grilled Comey kept trying to make it seem that Trump's pressure on Comey to drop the whole thing was benign, harmless and nothing illegal. They were just suggestions, not threats, just suggestions not intimidation. And there's nothing wrong with asking for loyalty. Their line of questioning is transparently evil. They know they are bad boys and that God knows they are sinning, but they don't care. A good fight is more important to them than good behavior.

One D senator asked the big question, what would have been the result if you HAD given into pressure. Comey replied that *the instigation into the Russia connection would have come to a halt, pure and simple.*

The entire American democracy would have been tottering in the balance if Comey had given in to that fascist totalitarian pig.

Comey looks bad for admitting how he leaked his memos to the press. Trump people just grab on to minor victories in the testimony and ignore the major defeats: The fact the Comey agreed that one *New York Times* story attacking Trump was basically false.

So never mind the 300 Times articles that ripped Trump, were on the money, and he never even tried to refute.

No, what counts is that one knee-jerk pro-Trump Senator focused on that one story and forced Comey to admit that it was false. That has one 100th of an ounce to do with the big picture at these hearings,

Trump's brainwashed son went nuts Tweeting that 'see, it IS all fake news. See?' All trials have points for the prosecution and the defense. The judgment is based on the big picture, not forcing the court to focus on only one exculpatory face. So what if one NYT Times story is wrong?

Huckabee's off-centered daughter, the bottom of the barrel of spokespeople, stood that the podium defiantly asserting that President Trump is not a liar and she is "frankly offended at the suggestion."

He lies more often than he tells the truth. One in a million people are that bad. It is sick in the head lying.

Paul Ryan, who sucks, stood at the microphones the other day and explained Trump pressuring Comey with "Don't forget, Trump is new at this."

Unreal. Learn as you go while in command of the nukes. If he was THAT new, then maybe he shouldn't have run. That's what happens when you turn the White House into Ted Mack's Amateur Hour.

Trump has his core of lobotomized guards who will support a clearly horrible man, no matter what. But the Russia stuff, and the constant small behavior, is starting to chip away at the edges. He might be dropping slowly but the trend is down. He's holding steady at 38% core support, Two months later he's holding steady at 37% core support. One month after, it's down to 36%. If it drops to 30% he's in a lot of trouble.

He so obviously in cahoots with the Russians it's ridiculous. He never ever says anything bad about them.

Now there is talk that the Russians have some dirt on Trump regarding some hookers. Let's see where these red white and blue Trump-lovers stand when it's revealed that he had sex with some 14 year old Russian girl and paid 15,000 rubles. Something like that would cut his fan base a bit.

The media keeps dragging out all the mummies from Watergate on TV shows. John Dean, Carl Bernstein, and a few others are all weighing in, and with one exception, they all say this is far worse than Watergate and this is just the tip of the iceberg. They also mention that at least Nixon was shrewd enough to make nice with some groups in his war chest, while Trump just seems to want to antagonize everybody, friend, foe and neutral alike. He's only happy when he's hurting someone.

NOT UNLESS THEY WANT ME

Trump is supposed to be visiting England soon, but now he is having second thoughts. He wants Prime Minister May to guarantee that there won't be protest demonstrations against him ... as if she can guarantee that. Now he might not go.

You bet there will be demonstrations.

Meanwhile his simple son made a strong case that his Dad really was trying to pressure Comey to do as he's told. Junior said what Trump has been trying not to say:

"When Trump tells you to do something, guess what, there's no ambiguity in it. You do your job."

His macho talk instinct and reflex got the best of him. That was not a smart thing to say, not when the President shoos everyone out of the Oval Office and tries to pressure Comey into dropping the Russia

Investigation, and people are talking about obstruction of justice and potential impeachment.

Trump and his kids say the same thing every time, no matter what they do wrong. "It's a witch hunt."

You bet it is; a righteous one. Unlike Salem, this time the accused actually are guilty of witchcraft. They have summoned the dark forces to try and rule a good country.

Most of Trump's TV expert defenders are slimebuckets, but even when they make a legitimate point in his defense, I don't care. Trump is so corrupt and evil that I hope he is always on his heels, and never get the chance to implement his totalitarian goals.

JEFF SESSESSIONS

Attorney General Jeff Sessions testified before a Senate hearing. The nation was glued to the TV set like the moon landing.

He said little that was enlightening, and furiously denied that there was any collusion with the Russians.

The real question for me is, why is he not doing his job as Attorney General and pursuing the investigation into Russian tampering with the elections of 2016, which is now a fact the Russians do not even deny?

Doesn't matter if Jeff is guilty of any wrongdoing or not! All I know is, this all American guy is the Attorney General and he is taking not one initiative into investigating one of the worst political attacks ever made on this country.

Meanwhile some toilet named Alex Jones, who everyone knows of except me, is calling for Trump to take military action to take this country back before the liberal coup takes over the government. I can't keep track of all these left wing and right wing dingbats. They are just people using politics to get rich and famous, and people fall for it. They are incendiary, per se.

Trump keeps tweeting that Comey is a bad guy for leaking, but even if so, he is no "nutcase." James is slick; he is no "whack job." He is a sophisticated man, and how dare you tell the Russian Ambassador that our FBI director is a real whack job and you had to fire him because he's nuts. What kind of FBI would not make sure that their leader was at least sane? Trump, you revolting man, you are more hated that all the other politicians in the history of this country combined.

JUNE 14 - SCALISE AND QATAR

A Republican Congressman was shot while playing baseball on a Wednesday morning in Virginia.

The shooter was a Bernie Sanders left wing extremist, but don't say that in public or else you'll get in a lot of trouble.

Congressman Steve Scalise, of Louisiana, the Majority Whip, was taking grounders at second base when he was shot near the hip. He was taken to the hospital in critical condition, but survived. The next day he pleaded for everyone to tone down the rhetoric.

Tell your boss to. He's the one that started up all the hatred and he did so from the time he entered the race in the summer of 2015.

Capital Police were there for the morning baseball practice by the Republican baseball team. The politicians were getting ready for the annual charity game between Democrats and Republicans. The shooter was a loser who lived in a van, and was often reported to the police for myriad infractions. Capitol police saved many lives that day and two of them were wounded. Jeff Flake, who was there, said that if not for the Capitol cops, "it would have been a massacre." Five others besides Congressman Scalise were wounded. The shooter, whose name we shall never remember, tried to hide behind the third base dugout, but went down in a hail of bullets, and was DOA at the hospital.

Bernie Sanders of course denounced this, and all acts of violence. Trump does the same thing when a right wing nut shoots people. The difference is that Sanders means it.

Trump, in June, sold 12 billion dollars worth of F-15 fighter jets to Qatar, a small country in the Arabian Gulf. A lot of people are furious with him for this, but the request was made during Obama's time and Trump is merely choosing not to stop it. Makes sense to me. Qatar is a U.S. ally. The U.S. has 10,000 troops there and more than one air base. This new deal means that the U.S. increases its air strength in the region without having to pay for the planes, and with plausible denial if Qatar wants to go after some terrorists on its own. The F-15 with Qatar markings are virtual U.S. planes, and Qatar can afford it.

Now everyone is screaming because Trump Twitted something against Qatar a few weeks ago and now he's selling arms to it.

Steve Scalise went through several surgeries and improved to stable after hanging on for dear life.

The annual softball game between Republicans and Democrats at National Stadium usually draws about 8,000 people, but the game on June 14 drew 24,000 people and was the lead story on the national news.

Trump is clearly under investigation now for obstruction of justice and there are already rumors that he is going to fire Mueller and the special investigative counsel. He's just going to keep firing people who are trying to prove he is in cahoots with the fucking Russians. Representative Adam Schiff of California is speaking out, warning Trump that if he fires Mueller there is going to be a Congressional revolt.

The things that a million Americans post about him on social media every day are amazingly vile hateful and disrespectful. What's worse, I love reading every one of them. I only subscribe on Facebook to anti-Trump groups. He is the worst pig of all time.

LONDON FIRE PROTEST - JUNE 16, 2017

A 24-story modern building in West London went up in flames and more than 70 people died.

Two days later, thousands of demonstrators marched in London protesting that the government did not do enough in response!

When is this insanity going to end? All the demonstrators are in love with themselves. We care so much! I care so much! What's wrong with you that you don't care like I do?

It's the social event of the demonstration that drives the demonstration, not the cause. It's a party. It's a gathering. That's what humans love to do. It can be a birthday party or a super bowl, or a walk to raise awareness for some cause. But the get-together itself is the definition of the situation, not the issue involved. Black Lives Matter is a party, a social event; don't kid yourself, No one likes to be bored. People love company and get-togethers. Just because it's based around being angry about something does not change that dynamic.

Meanwhile, Trump keeps Tweeting offensive remarks and incriminating remarks, and all his advisers are begging him to stop.

He can't stop and he won't stop.

WARM BEER

Otto Warmbier was a 22 year-old American tourist who went to North Korea in 2015. In his hotel room, he stole a political banner to take home as a souvenir. Only in North Korea would a political banner be in one's hotel to begin with.

Warmbier was caught with the loot and sentenced to a long prison term. While in custody, the North Koreans beat him badly, causing brain damage and putting him into a coma.

The North Koreans finally released his comatose body in June, and, shortly after he came home, he died.

Trump, instead of directing rage against North Korea, instead Tweeted anger at former President Obama: "If he were brought home sooner, I think the results would have been a lot different."

Yes, but what are you doing in response now?

Trump granted trade concessions to China (agreeing not to impose pending ones) in exchange for cooperation on the Warm Beer man. Trump Tweets gently that "Cooperation with China on this obviously hasn't worked out." Big tough guy talk against China all throughout the campaign and then, when it's crunch time, he plays it safe.

I can spend all day reading new essays from great people condemning Trump for his arrogance, stupidity, insanity, racism, corruption, and badly articulated thoughts. But why bother? I knew he was an evil insane sack of trash after I watched the first two Republican Debates. I could believe that he was still in the Republican field after the way he misbehaved like a 6 year old who was immature for a 6 year old. He was done with me so long ago as a total scum that I can't lose too much time reading about how everyone else is saying how bad he is. Yeah. No kidding.

New Senatorial charges are being raised by Democrats based on his violations of all ethics laws by not disconnecting from business that are gaining financially from the help of his presidency.

Trump keeps appearing on my social media pages pitching a chance to meet him and have a photo taken with him for large sums of money! I'd spit on mine and tear it up.

There are now several angles from where people are closing in on him. The details are complex, but for starters, General Mike Flynn is going to go to prison, and he might get a suspended sentence if he cooperates by telling the truth about Trump.

The latest inside gossip is that Trump wants out! He wants to resign! But he knows it's not an option for his ego. All he wants to do is golf.

This man is supposed to be the one person in the country who must put the interests of others above himself, and all he does is watch TV and Tweet nasty things about anyone who criticizes him.

Two days ago the White House announced that from now on, press conferences can no longer be recorded in audio or video! Unreal! You can walk in and listen to what a spokesliar says (the coward rarely takes questions personally) but you can't tape it! Reporters were flipping out, and losing their cool when discussing this on their respective networks.

It's getting dangerous, and now there is contact in the skies of the Middle East over Syria between U.S. and Russian supplied Syrian jets. When his presidency is close to falling, he will start a war.

SPECIAL ELECTION ON GEORGIA

It's been the talk of the TV for a week. Georgia is having a special election for a vacated Congressional seat. It's going to be a close one. Can the Dems upset the Trump train by taking over a traditional Republican district? CNN had two day countdown clocks to the closing of the polls in that Georgia district, a cheesy move.

Turns out the Republican won a close race and the Democrats took it very hard. It was impossible to find the basics of what happened the next day because all the stories were reaction, analysis, predictions and proselytizing. The basics of reporting were not even involved on any website at all!

I had to go to Wikipedia to find the basics.

It's like that with everything. If a team wins the championship and you don't follow that sport closely but you're curious, good luck finding the basics of who won what! It's all analysis, predictions, angry or happy rants. Takes all day to find out who won in how many games.

The news media is so bad now it's hard to watch. It's all about preaching and pontificating, not reporting.

The winner was Karen Handel in Georgia and the loser was Jon Ossoff. Trump held a We-Love-Trump rally to celebrate.

All he does is makes speeches to sycophants as if the campaign were still on for his election. It's sick.

Ossof the loser is a 30 year old documentary film maker. Maybe the Dems should have come up with a stronger candidate. In any case, they made it close, 51-49 in a very Republican district, so why the panic weeping aftermath by the Dems? Ya did good.

NO TAPES

June 22: Trump finally made an official statement about the secret tapes of him and James Comey in the Oval Office. He said there are no tapes. Yet he had tried to intimidate Comey by suggesting in a Tweet that there were tapes. For 40 days the Congress has been trying to get an answer on whether there is or is not a taping system in the White House where people are being recorded without their knowledge. A lot of work has gone into this and Chump in Chief keeps dropping vague hints like "I'll make a statement on that soon."

He is the biggest jerk that ever lived.

Now he is in the process of repealing Obamacare. He had promised to do it immediately, and is making statement that "I never said that, you can examine my speeches and you will find that I never said that." Just watch the video clips of him saying those exact words over and over.

It's taking very long to try and get this repeal done, and it's not done on June 23, yet he claimed on the campaign trail over and over that as soon as he gets in he's going to end Obamacare and do it quickly and it will be easy. "Believe me, believe me, it will be done very quickly." Now it's five months in and even four Republican Senators are opposed to it. Yet he keeps saying "I never said we could do it quickly." Cut to 12 clips of him saying that.

I would not want him to be my next-door neighbor. There was a "President Obama." There is a Donald Trump. He is not my president.

Millions feel the same way. Never has ONE PERSON in US history brought out the worst in everybody, including me. Trump is an evil man. He has no decency, and now it's common knowledge that he is a liar. The fourth-rate talent he has around him is pathetic, at least at the press spokesperson position. He is beyond redemption. I live to see him dead.

The Congress is not through with the tapes business. They are going to continue investigating and not take his word for it. Trump and his blind followers think it's all amusing. I do not.

Meanwhile Trump has refused to hold an official celebration of Ramadan at the White House, ending a tradition. I have no problem with Trump on this one. We can respect the Muslim faith without bowing down to it with token ceremonies lacking sincerity.

JUNE 27, 2017

Trump is finally admitting that Russia meddled in the election, so he is changing the subject to why didn't Obama do something about it if he knew it was happening. Trump is demanding an apology from the Obama Administration for allowing the Russian meddling to happen. And this after he insisted for a month that it never happened. Now he's focusing on Robert Mueller being too close to Comey to be objective in the investigation. Does Trump think he can find an FBI replacement that was not close to Comey?

MIKA BRZEZINSKI

She is the co-host of MSNBC's Morning Joe TV show and Trump is having a Tweet fight with her. He tweeted that he had wanted to come down for an interview but "she was bleeding badly from a face lift. I said no!"

There are no photos of her bleeding from the face and it was really a way to tell everyone that she's had facial surgery, as if he hasn't.

Then the two hosts said that Trump's people tried to threaten/ blackmail them with a *National Enquirer* story about them. If they would call Trump and apologize and agree to desist in their attacks on him, then he would get his friend the Enquirer to kill the story.

Trump is tweeting that she is dumb as a rock.

It's all abuse and woman-bashing. Many Republicans are condemning the statements, and condemning many of his recent hate tweets.

Meanwhile sorry Sarah Huckabee stands at the podium and says, "Too bad. This is a man who when he's attacked, will hit back ten times harder."

What justification is there for that? No one but a lunatic thug thinks 10-1 is a fair response. She thinks that's presidential. How about ignoring personal attacks and getting to work on something.

WRESTLER

July 1, 2017: Donald Trump Tweeted a video of a wrestling match in which the winner smacks the loser senseless, and at the end you see that the loser is wearing CNN logos.

People are angry and Trump's defenders are saying it's all a joke and we should all laugh along.

As if Trump has a sense of humor! As if he's ever laughed. (No one has ever seen him laugh). All of a sudden we're supposed to laugh along. He can NEVER take a joke. All of a sudden it's just silly.

That was a clear incitement to violence against the media. Whatever they report, he just calls it fake news. His defenders suck!

TURNS OUT

A few days later it turns out that the man who made this violent video of Trump beating up a CNN wrestler has made several very racist videos that were already going around right wing sites. The man issued an apology saying none of it was intended to be racist; but it obviously was.

July 5, and Trump is off to Europe to get away from the Russia story at home. He's going to meet Vladimir Putin, one-on-one, for the first time. Or is he?

This G-20 Summit is expected to draw thousands of European protesters with nothing useful to say, screaming things at the top of their lungs and throwing stuff.

North Korea celebrated the Fourth by launching its most successful ballistic missile to date. Trump is asking China to step in and do something about North Korea. This is getting scary, with my nephew in Korea driving a tank.

PUTIN CLEARS THE AIR

Vlad Putin told reporters today that yes, Donald Trump did ask him if Russia meddled in the election of 2016, and Putin said that Trump seemed to accept his answer that Russia did not.

Since the Russians obviously were trying to get Trump elected in 2016, this whole theater show is an insult to the world's intelligence, and to the intelligence community.

Putin did make a little joke while sitting next to Trump, asking if these are the same reporters that are criticizing you, and Putin laughed at his own joke. It actually seemed affectionate, not vicious towards Trump, more of an icebreaker than a jab. What was interesting to me was to see Putin genuinely laugh. It was controlled, and he didn't hee-haw out loud, but it was more than I have ever seen Trump laugh.

JUNIOR DEAL

So now it is revealed that Trump Jr. had a secret meeting with a Russian lawyer back in June that he failed to tell anyone about during a year of investigation when he claims to have been cooperative.

Trump was in Poland where he complained, seated beside the Polish Prime Minister, that "CNN has been fake news for a long time."

Historian Douglas Brinkley said on TV that Britain and Germany didn't want him to visit, and that the riots everywhere he goes are a nightmare. Only Poland wanted him to visit at all.

PUTIN'S OFFER

The news is focused for days in mid-July on the meeting at Trump Tower in March 2016 between Trump Jr., several of Trump's closest people, and a Russian lawyer. The meeting was held so that a foreign government, an avowed long time enemy of the USA could deliver dirt on Hillary Clinton.

Trump Jr. denied any such meeting until records proved it, and then he got ahead by releasing e-mails about the meeting before CNN did.

Trumps latest mouthpiece on all the channels Sekelew or whatever his name is, is left with two points he clings to: 1 - No laws were violated. What laws were violated? Two: How does this compare the something Hillary Clinton did?

On the second point, stop acting like you're six years old. For one thing, she's not so important right now. Plus it's apples and oranges; two different subjects.

On his other point, well some Democrats think that a few laws that have indeed been violated and they will act on this fact, no matter how angry and glib his lawyer sounds. And even if none have been violated, the fact that Jr. and other lied over and over about no such meeting makes it serious. Trump's approval rating is now 36% which is a new low for him. Donald of course is claiming that he had no knowledge of this meeting with the Russians. His son and virtually all of his inner circle celebrity names were there at a nine-person meeting; they have the dirt on his opponent; Donald is the most thin-skinned and vindictive person on earth; and somehow he had no idea that this meeting had ever taken place.

A foreign government was trying to influence an American election and the Trump defenders say it's all Russia-mania "fake news."

Meanwhile Vladimir Putin is offering to provide transcripts of what was said at the meeting. Gee, what a flawlessly honest source that would be; and what an arrogant gesture. Don still never ever says a bad word about Russia, although some sanctions are kicking in and making the Russians angry.

G-20

Now it is revealed that Putin and Trump had a secret meeting at the G-20 Summit of more than 20 minutes (more I think) and they had tried to keep it secret. Then there's a video of a dinner where Trump and Putin are some distance apart and are communicating with hand-signals like a husband and wife with pet rituals. Sickening.

More and more details keep coming out about the March 2016 meeting with the Russians over the dirt on Hillary. Trump Jr.'s defenders say he was naive and new at all this, yet Junior told the Russians right away that he wanted them to hold back on revealing the dirt until just before the election. Junior is not very innocent and naive.

The NY Times now says that Paul Manifort was in debt to Russian bankers by 17 million dollars when he first took over the Trump campaign.

SESSIONS RIPPED

Trump shocked me when I heard the clip of him tearing into his attorney general.

Trump is also openly saying that the FBI Director should report to him personally and not to the Department of Justice. Sieg Heil!

July 21 and the country is stunned by his behavior. He now is trying to gather personal dirt on anyone who is involved in the investigation into him and Russia, and he warned Special Investigator Mueller to watch his step when it comes to checking into his personal finances. He is really warning Mueller that he has no right to look into his tax returns and to other things, when the whole investigation is based around money deals. All the TV experts say that the special investigator has every right and a duty to look into Trump's tax returns.

BOY SCOUTS - ATTACKS ON SESSIONS - JULY 24-7, 2017

Trump gave a speech to a rally of Boy Scouts in West Virginia. He had promised in advance in writing not to turn it into a political speech. He did. It was horrible. He bashed President Obama, Hillary Clinton, and the media. He praised himself, claiming that "I can act more presidential than any President with the exception of the late Abraham Lincoln."

The late Abraham Lincoln? He's been dead for 150 years you DUMMY.

You "can" act more presidential? Anyone "can" climb Mount Everest.

He knew how to play to the crowd. He got a lot of cheers and made them boo Obama, which they were happy to do, but it was a crowd control game. There was a lot of backlash from Boy Scout members, in writing, the following day, but they couldn't stop the power of the spoken word at a mass rally. Dictator Don knew how to exploit that.

He is the only president that has a campaign rally that never ends.

Meanwhile DT keeps attacking and criticizing Attorney General, Jeff Session on Twitter and in interviews. It's incredible, and totally transparent. He doesn't want to face the blowback from firing him, so he is trying to intimidate him into resigning, and Sessions will not. I know of no instance in American history when a president has even criticized his own attorney general, let alone attacked him persistently in an obvious attempt to humiliate him into resigning.

Sessions-Trump was a scary combo and all agree that no one was more loyal to Trump than Sessions throughout the controversial campaign. And now he just hurls abuse on him. Everyone is watching this horror show in awe and disgust. Trump stands at podiums and keeps saying that Sessions needs to do a better job on this and on that, and no one has ever seen anything like it.

Trump told the Wall Street Journal that *"Well Jeff Session was a guy who saw that we were drawing 40,000 people at our rallies and he thought he'd get on the bandwagon. It wasn't a big deal when I picked up his endorsement, and frankly his help didn't make any difference."* There is no truth to that. Sessions was important and didn't lust for power in a Trump Administration. He was asked to join, and never begged. Trump is lying, as he always does. Trump thinks he can keep tearing up the parking tickets and not have to eventually pay the price.

Most Republicans are defending Jeff Sessions, saying that he is doing a good job and shouldn't be criticized.

McCain came out of the hospital in a dramatic scene, just so he could vote to make sure that 23 million people lose their health insurance (July 23).

As for Trump, it's all about the Russia investigation and his secret tax returns, and what the Russians are blackmailing him with. He wants to keep shooting the detective that suspects him in the robbery. I think he is stupid and his followers are stupider. He won on the stupidizing of this country through crap TV. 10% of his supporters can speak and sound vaguely intelligent at the same time.

SCARY MOOCH

The new White House Communications Director is a man who refers to himself as "The Mooch" His real name is Anthony Scaramucci and he is supposed to be here to help with communications. All he's doing is creating ugly new controversies.

Tony gave a recorded interview in which he attacked two of the men closes to Trump, men on his same team. He called White House Chief of Staff, Reince Preibus a "f______g paranoid schizophrenic" and worse than that, and he said of Steve Bannon, the man who got Trump elected. "I'm not like Steve Bannon who sucks his own c__k."

There's plenty more where that came from. Scaramucci talked of "c__k-blocking" this person and that.

Trump continues to attack and humiliate Jeff Sessions, and is obviously forcing him to resign so he can hire someone obedient and loyal during the Congressional recess. That new person will then fire Mueller and appoint a Trump-friendly special prosecutor.

In the meantime, Trump has never said a bad word about Putin.

Trump is the ONLY ONE who is claiming that Russia did not interfere in the 2016 Election.

REINCE PREIBUS OUT

Big mouth Scaramucchi got his way. He bad mouthed the White House Chief of Staff and forced Preibus to step down. Johnny Kelly has taken his place. Scaramucci's wife has filed for divorce over her husband's enabling of Trump. There are stories about "Trump divorces." I totally get it.

The Senate is trying to draft a bill forbidding the President to fire special counsel Mueller. Many major newspapers now are saying that the bottom is starting to fall out and it might be over soon for this presidency.

TOO MOOCH TOO SOON

The first thing the new Chief of Staff, John F. Kelly did was fire Scaramucci. President Trump backed the decision, saying that some of

Scaramucci's comments were inappropriate. When Trump thinks you've gone too far with your comments, you're in trouble.

Nee revelations are that Trump instructed Trump Jr. on what to say in his sworn deposition on the Russia meetings. Some are calling for criminal charges for obstruction of justice.

Trump is claiming he got a phone call from the President of Mexico congratulating him on the new tighter border security. Mexico said no such phone call took place.

Trump said that the Boy Scouts said that his was the greatest speech ever delivered to the Boy Scouts. The Boys Scouts later issued a statement that they never said that.

When reporters asked Sarah Huckabee Sanders about Trump's lies she got indignant and said 'That's a pretty bold accusation.' So? So what if it is? That's no response. You still owe us a response, rather than suggest that categorizing the charge is somehow a response to it. It's the truth. Trump lies ten times a day and you get all offended when a reporter uses the L-word?

Transcripts of Trump's first telephone conversation with the President of Mexico have been released are causing a stir.

Trump is trying to bully Nieto, the President of Mexico, on the telephone, asking, almost demanding, that Nieto stop saying Mexico will not pay for the wall. Trump is telling him that we can work it out so that it "comes out in the wash." Mexico won't really pay for it, with the help of some maneuverings, but he should stop saying it because it's "hurting me politically."

As if the President of Mexico is supposed to care about Trump's political situation. The President of Mexico kept trying to explain to Trump that it was a matter of Mexican pride and Trump just didn't get it.

Amazing. And then he was just as loony with a conversation with the President of Australia.

It was wrong for someone to leak these transcripts and it proves that people close to Trump are against him and are willing to undermine him. It might be someone real close!

He snapped angrily at the Prime Minister of Australia that "This is the most unpleasant conversation I've had all day. Talking to Putin earlier today was pleasant." Then he virtually hung up on him. The president of my country is a revolting pig!

Trump finally signed the sanctions against Russia bill that had sat on his desk for three days unsigned while he pouted because he hated to betray his ally by doing something in favor of the United States.

He signed it, but immediately criticized it. Then he had the audacity to Tweet that "US-Russia relations have reached a dangerous point now and a new low because of Congress."

He was dis-owning the bill he had signed, and threatening the world with nuclear destruction because he did not get his way. Most Congresspersons protested this statement, including many Republicans. Then the Russian Prime Minister chimes in that Congress is undermining the power of the Executive Branch.

Mind your own business. This is my country, not yours; what business is it of yours whether our system of government is not to your liking because you didn't get your nefarious plan through, this time.

AUGUST 6, 2017

Christ Christie admitted that the March 2016 meeting with the Russians at Trump Tower was a bad idea.

Trump gave a speech to a pack of morons in West Virginia in which he said "The Russia investigation is a total fabrication." There is not one shred of evidence to back him up. How could investigators make up the thing they are investigating?

Then he mockingly asks his crowd of pinheads: "Have you seen any Russians in West Virginia? Are there any Russians here?"

As if that has anything to do with anything! How is that relevant in any way?

Republican Senator Jeff Flake (AZ) is now all over the TV, politely separating himself from Trump. Flake emphasizes the right point repeatedly, that all of Trump's insults are serious matters and have undermined his presidency completely. Insulting people solves nothing.

The worst human being in the history of the USA is in charge.

I hope to God he is impeached. I pray that he goes away.

Every day, Donald Trump tells more vicious lies than I have ever told in my entire life. Everyone who knows me respects my integrity and honesty. I have faults, but being a MALICIOUS LIAR is not one of them. Donald J. Trump is everything the Trump haters say he is.

MANAFORT RAIDED - AUGUST, 2017

The FBI shook up the Trump team when it raided the home of his former campaign manager Paul Manafort. All of the CNN pundits see this as really serious stuff. This shows that the FBI won't be intimidated by Trump and that they feel that Manafort is not fully cooperating with investigators. A judge has to have some powerful evidence to authorize such a raid on a person's home, especially the home of a man so powerful and important.

Trump is in a frightening war of threats with Kim Jong Un of North Korea.

[Now here, in 2020, I have to make a major interjection, because I thought I had written, back in 2017, about something important. I guess talked to a few people about it, but didn't write it down. It ties in with the last sentence above and the incident below.

The North Korean dictator kept threatening Trump and the USA with missile attack and over-flights of Guam. Sometimes he spoke of hitting Guam. He reminded the world that he could hit Seattle, and soon, any city in America. It was humiliating to my pride to read of these threats to strike US soil with missiles. I was reaching the point where I was thinking, 'Go ahead and try it, moth______r.' Stop the threats, and let's see action … <u>you big mouth</u>!'

Trump was at a table with some people and reporters asked him about it and he said, "You don't threaten the United States like that. If he tries anything …" I don't have the rest of the exact quote handy now, but I liked it; and I liked it a lot. It was close to what I was thinking. For once I felt like Trump was my president.

The world held its breath to see what NK would do.

Kim backed off! He made up a lame excuse why the overflight of Guam that he was threatening had to be postponed. It was a huge story and Trump's best day, and his best move. The bully from North Korea had met his match.

Then, just when the headlines should have been singing the praise of Trump for winning the showdown of threats - that had been building for three presidencies - Charlottesville happened. The timing could not have been worse for Trump.

He could have said a few brief not-incendiary comments about Charlottesville and directed the subject to Korea. Instead he made terrible statements about Charlottesville while I was trying to yell at him through the TV to keep your big mouth shut about that and focus on this monumental achievement in foreign policy. But instead, his greatest day was totally cancelled out by Charlottesville. Two thirds of the country screamed at him for his words, and forgot completely what had just happened in Korea. – MD 2020]

AUGUST 12, 2017

Charlottesville white rednecks have held two demonstrations, partly protesting the removal of the statues of Confederate war heroes. There were counter-demonstrations on August 12 and violence erupted. It was racists versus lefties in the streets and the video was all over CNN. Trump made a statement that we must prevent this kind of hatred and violence, "on many sides, on many sides."

David Duke tweeted in response, "I would recommend you take a good look in the mirror & remember it was White Americans who put you in the presidency, not radical leftists."

That is certainly true, and in one of the most horrible moments in TV history, in September of 2016, Donald Trump denied that he had even heard of David Duke, and denied it repeatedly.

One of the Charlottesville rednecks, a 20 year from Ohio, drove his car into a crowd of "counter-protesters," and killed a 34 year old woman. It was murder, an act of Confederate terrorism. When Trump said, "on many sides, on many sides" he really upset the entire country, including me.

I wish the counter-protesters hadn't shown up and made the whole thing such a sensation. I don't think they are entirely peaceful. But the white supremacists are the problem, not the counter-protesters, and what Trump said was disgusting, Republicans and Democrats both condemned his failure to call the white supremacists out.

Trump spent 18 months condemning Obama and the Democrats for not using the term "Islamic terrorism." Call it what it is. Now the whole world is outraged because the hypocrite won't use the term "white supremacist." That's because he is one, and two different writers insist that as a young man, Trump was obsessed with Hitler. So he knows what a white supremacist is.

VP Pence said the words, "we condemn white supremacists," but Trump won't as of August 13, so we'll see.

[The comment that really hurt was when DJT said that there were "good people on both sides" not him saying you had bad people on both sides. It's the same point either way, but praising the neo-Nazis as "good people" was the big bomb.]

AUGUST 16-17, 2017

Shepherd Smith of FOX News announced yesterday that for the first time, not one Republican, or conservative commentator would agree to come on the show and side with Trump over what he said about Charlottesville. Smith said that this is a big TV station and most of the time, conservatives are competing to get on; but this is a first.

There was a terrorist attack in Barcelona, Spain. Some born loser drove a truck into a crowd.

Trump Tweeted an insane story he had told on the campaign trail in 2016 about Black Jack Pershing, and how that famous American WWI hero took care of terrorism in the Philippines. Trump said that Pershing executed Muslims; using bullets dipped in pig's blood, and buried them next to pigs.

The follow up Tweet read, "Study what General Pershing of the United States did to terrorists when caught. There was no more Islamic terror for 35 years!"

Study?

All sources have debunked this story as false, and the second part is off-base because Islamic terrorism wasn't a major problem, one way or another, in 1917.

Smith (my hope that maybe FOX isn't all corrupt) just shook his head and said, "So that's how our president weighed in on this today."

At least Jeffrey Lord got fired from CNN for sending someone a sarcastic 'Seig Heil.' Great!

I've done that, but I'm a stand-up comedian and a freelance writer, plus I watch my step on social media and in e-mails. I also don't work for the hypersensitive, politically correct CNN. I'm also attacking the right when I do it, and Lord was attacking his critics on the left. For right-wing Trump-lover to invoke 'Seig Heil' in anger is a thematic contradiction.

In today's PC atmosphere, you can't joke around like that if you have a corporate paycheck. Lord elected Donald Trump by holding his own on CNN against all comers throughout the campaign of 2016. I saw him talk for 12 hours.

BANNON OUT AT LAST

Unabashed racist White House Chief Strategist, Steve Bannon finally got sacked on August 18, 2017. The DNC released a statement. 'There is one less white supremacist in the White House, but there is still the one that counts behind the Resolute Desk.'

The CEO of Fox, Robert Murdoch, announced in August 17 that he was donating one million dollars to an anti-defamation league. That is serious news. The right-wing network that elected Trump is donating a million dollars to the opposition! That's how bad things are for racist Trump. He is isolated, or at least that's what they say.

The number of Republicans denouncing Trump is increasing. There is talk of Trump being "primaried," meaning the Republican voters will be presented a choice whether to make him the nominee for re-election in 2020.

The thought of eight years of this monster is too much to bear!

"BLOOD AND SOIL"

"Blood and soil!" was the slogan that the racists of Charlottesville chanted.

Racial purity is the 'blood' component of that slogan. But here is where the neo-Nazis are not just malicious, they are fools. They have this big thing about the white race and white power. Okay, we read you. But why are you invoking Hitler? He and the Nazis didn't stand for the white race, they stood for the <u>German</u> race. That was it. How many of these Charlotte-heads were white, but not German? Please step out of the line. Why are you here? Hitler wouldn't have stood up for you at all.

The entire 'Aryan' thing was strictly German. It wasn't White with the capital w. Until late in the 1800's, the Europeans were considered one race, with branches within. Then along came a couple of famous German writers who wrote phenomenal best-sellers introducing the idea that all whites were not created equal. Some whites are superior to others. The German 'Aryan' strain was superior to other white European people. These ideas took hold and that's how the Nazis became such racists: <u>against fellow white people</u>. - So the Neo-Nazis are idiots because, except for any pure Germans in that tiki-torch march, the Nazis consider you an inferior. - Most Jews are not technically European, but most of them look pretty white to me. Hitler looked down on Greeks, Irish, Poles, and they seem fairly white to me. What color are the Russians, the folk that Hitler tried to exterminate? - The real reason those tiki people chanted against the Jews was because they didn't dare come out and chant against what they were really against, which was black people - They knew the blacklash would be a loser - So throw this American Jewish minority under the bus, to avoid clashing directly with the much larger minority, and the one which has more national support – Besides, the Jews will probably just scratch their head and say, "When did we suddenly become the big problem all over again? At what point were we ever the #1 racial issue in the United States to begin with?" - So the tiki-gods were quite clever breaking out the Jewish thing, and the foot soldiers were fools for falling for it and marching to slogans that made absolutely no sense.

BANNON DEFIANT

Ousted racist Steve Bannon is announcing that he going to go to war against those still within the White House that he feels are not good for America - which means those who got him fired.

My town of Boston was the main focus of the national news on Saturday Aug 19, 2017. A follow up right-wing rally (to the Charlottesville affair) took place. The media built it up like the solar eclipse.

It turns out that only about 100 right-wing troublemakers showed up, and about 100,000 counter-protesters were there to meet them.

The skinheads didn't dare try and start any violence or else they would have been stomped. Made be proud to be a Bostonian.

AUGUST 21, 2017

Trump addressed the nation on Afghanistan. After Tweeting for years how the U.S. had to get out and it was a horrible war, and after pledging to get out during the campaign for President, Trump told the nation that there will be no withdrawals and some new troops would be sent there, but he won't say how many. That is classified.

THE END OF VOLUME ONE

APPENDIX - TRUMP TAPPER - ARIZONA JUDGE INTERVIEW – JUNE 2016

TRUMP: I'll tell you what it has to do. I've had ruling after ruling after ruling that's been bad rulings, OK? I've been treated very unfairly. Before him, we had another judge. If that judge was still there, this case would have been over two years ago.

Let me just tell you, I've had horrible rulings, I've been treated very unfairly by this judge. Now, this judge is of Mexican heritage. I'm building a wall, OK? I'm building a wall. I am going to do very well with the Hispanics, the Mexicans —

TAPPER: So, no Mexican judge could ever be involved in a case that involves you?

TRUMP: Well, he's a member of a society, where — you know, very pro- Mexico, and that's fine. It's all fine but —

TAPPER: Except that you're calling into question his heritage.

TRUMP: I think he should recuse himself.

TAPPER: Because he's Latino?

TRUMP: Then, you also say, does he know the lawyer on the other side? I mean, does he know the lawyer? You know, a lot of people say —

TAPPER: But I'm not talking about that. I'm talking about —

TRUMP: That's another problem.

TAPPER: You're invoking his race talking about whether or not he can do his job.

TRUMP: Jake, I'm building a wall. OK? I'm building a wall. I'm trying to keep business out of Mexico. Mexico's fine.

TAPPER: But he's an American.

TRUMP: He's of Mexican heritage and he's very proud of it, as I am where I come from, my parents.

TAPPER: No?

TRUMP: No. He's proud of his heritage. I respect him for that.

TAPPER: But you're saying you can't do his job because of that.

TRUMP: Look, he's proud of his heritage, OK? I'm building a wall.

Now, I think I'm going to do very well with Hispanics because they are going to get jobs right now. They are going to get jobs. I think I'm going to do very well with Hispanics.

We are building a wall. He's a Mexican. We're building a wall between here and Mexico.

The answer is, he is giving us very unfair rulings, rulings that people can't even believe. This case should have ended years ago in summary judgment. The best lawyers I have spoken to so many lawyers, they said, this is not a case. This is a case that should have ended.

TAPPER: I —

TRUMP: This judge is giving us unfair rulings. Now, I say why? Well, I'm building a wall, OK? And it's a wall between Mexico. Not another country.

[end excerpt]

[2016 note] - The man is Gonzo! The judge he's accusing of prejudice is Gonzalo Curiel. This judge had done Trump a huge favor by pushing the Trump U trial forward to November 28, after the election. Trumps lawyers one month ago said he was doing his job and there was no plan to ask for a recusal.

Almost all the top Republicans are disowning this Trump position. Even Newt Gingrich a potential VP, is saying it is racist and inexcusable. Trump called a huge meeting and ordered his staff to keep attacking the judge. "The ones asking these questions are the racists," he told them. "Keep going after them."

All the thug tactics he's used as a thug businessman he thinks he can apply to the Presidential race. This time he may have really hurt himself. Most of the articles coming out about the Trump campaign are saying that it is chaotic and bizarre. No communications director. Just him Tweeting and reacting to criticism with attacks. No one on the staff knows how to represent his POV because he won't share it with them and he changes it so often. The other day he responded to a New York Time reporter's question with, "You're a real beaut."

https://www.cnn.com/2017/04/20/politics/donald-trump-gonzalo-curiel-jake-tapper-transcript/index.html

Above is the link address to a recent CNN recall of the interview.

Judge Curiel